D1562808

THE QUEST

Research and
Inquiry in
Arts Education

Richard Courtney

UNIVERSITY
PRESS OF
AMERICA

LANHAM • NEW YORK • LONDON

Copyright © 1987 by

University Press of America,® Inc.

4720 Boston Way
Lanham, MD 20706

3 Henrietta Street
London WC2E 8LU England

British Cataloging in Publication Information Available

Library of Congress Cataloging in Publication Data

Courtney, Richard.
    The quest : research & inquiry in arts education.

    Bibliography: p.
    Includes index.
    1. Arts—Study and teaching   2. Aesthetics—Study
and teaching.   I. Title.
NX280.C68   1987   700'.7   86-24693
ISBN 0-8191-5744-9 (alk. paper)
ISBN 0-8191-5745-7 (pbk. : alk. paper)

IN MEMORIAM

Three friends whose ideas have greatly
influenced my work in different ways:

H.MARSHALL McLUHAN

FREDERICK MAY

and

G.WILSON KNIGHT

iii

ACKNOWLEDGEMENTS

I am grateful to many people their invitations and their kindnesses, including in: Britain – Royal Society of Arts, Society for Teachers of Speech and Drama, and National Association for Teachers of Drama; Canada – the Universities of McGill, Calgary, Western Ontario, Toronto, Victoria, Montreal, Dalhousie, Simon Fraser and Ottawa, the Teachers' College, Truro, Nova Scotia, the Canadian Child and Youth Drama Association, the Canadian Society for Education Through Art, and the Council of Drama Education in Ontario; United States – the Universities of Washington, New Mexico, Arizona State, Brigham Young, California State at Northridge, U.C.L.A., the Aspen Institute, John F.Kennedy Centre (Washington, D.C.), Children's Theatre Association of America, American Theatre Association; in Australia – International Society for Education Through the Arts, Australian Arts Council, National Association for Drama in Education and branches, the Universities of Sydney, Melbourne, Macquarrie, Flinders, New South Wales, and Western Australia, Melbourne State College, Rusden College, the Drama Resource Centre (Victoria), Curriculum Development Centre in Canberra; and in Europe – the International Theatre Institute (UNESCO), University of Rome, and Centre des Cultures du Monde, Paris.

I wish to thank the agencies and institutions for which I have conducted research projects, including: Alberta Culture; Ontario Arts Council; Department of Education, Goverment of Ontario; Social Sciences & Humanities Research Council of Canada; Design Council, Department of Industry, Trade & Commerce, Government of Canada; National Institute of Education, Washington, D.C., and CEMREL, St.Louis; Department of Theatre Arts, University of New Mexico; Australian Council for the Arts; Drama Resource Centre, Melbourne State College, Melbourne, Australia; and the Ontario Institute for Studies in Education, Toronto.

I am grateful to the following colleagues for reading the manuscript and for their valuable comments: Drs. David Abbey, David Hunt, Howard Russell and Ian Winchester; to Co-Investigators Dr. Jack Morrison, Paul Park, David Booth, John Emerson and Natalie Kuzmich; to Research Officers Dr. Pamela Sturgess, Sandra Katz and Nikki Divito; and to my wife, Rosemary Courtney, for her considerable editorial assistance and the index.

R.C.

CONTENTS

PREFACE

This book is about the arts and the ways we can understand them. It aims to introduce ideas of research and inquiry into arts education to three groups: those beginning in the field, including thesis students; the supervisors of dissertations who wish to provide their candidates with an introduction to the main issues; and scholars in the field generally.

Study of the arts and aesthetic education has not been particularly successful in the past. This is an area of inquiry that is often elusive. Indeed, if we can successfully research in this field, we are likely to be so in other fields. Thus this book emphasizes the key ideas that lie behind research. Indeed, without them we may inadvertently let the important issues slip through the cracks of our categories.

I have used basic terminology in the following ways:

* "inquiry" is the various ways in which we address issues and problems ("the problematic");

* "scholarship" is a general address to the problematic that stresses a wealth of background knowledge and wisdom;

* "research" is a precise approach to the problematic which allows us to say, "this is the case."

Many parts of this book consist of sections of papers and lectures given in various parts of the world. In most cases, they were requested by my hosts and so they represent responses to genuine needs. In order to have a logical sequence to the book, I have severely edited and re-arranged the material.

R.C.
Toronto
1986

ix

CHAPTER 1

THE QUEST

"To imagine is everything"
                    - Einstein

        Our subject matter is how we can STUDY the arts
in education. This book specifically does not describe
how we create or appreciate the arts.

        Not that creating or appreciating the arts are
unimportant. Far from it. They are the kernel of what
we are about. The ability to imagine and to externalize
this in a medium is a uniquely human ability.

        Our quest here, however, is: How we can study the
relationship of arts and education? Are there "correct"
methods of inquiry? How do we conduct research in arts
education?

                    WHAT IS RESEARCH?

        What is research in this context? It is often
said that artists conduct research while they create
and, in a popular sense, this is true. Artists discover
new ways of knowing, use innovative methods to explore
meaning, and are on "the cutting edge" of the future.
They focus on the mental processes of imagining, seeing
possibilities, and then expressing them in action - in
an artistic medium during their life experience. That
is, artists engage in "experiential" inquiry: they find
new ways to explore knowledge as they create. This is
similar to how we operate in everyday life. It is also
like such techniques as "the experiential workshop" and
human activity in general. What makes artists different
is the medium in which their exploration takes occurs -
their art.

        Professional researchers, however, have a more
limited view of the term, "research." In arts education
they may study the creators, appreciators, teachers and
learners of the arts to find out if what they are doing
is effective. In other words, researchers usually try
to distance themselves from the event; they attempt to
be objective, or dispassionate, about it. They regard
themselves more as scientists than as artists. They say

1

that research is more of a science than it is an art. How can we reconcile these statements?

In fact, both views are true. The artist and the scientist have their own ways to discover knowledge and meaning. Neither is better or worse than the other. Rather, they complement each other. Indeed, some modern researchers have devised methods that attempt to give scientific validity to more experiential approaches. They recognize that the most rigid objective methods, used by mechanical scientists, cannot always capture the elusive quality of human nature. Despite the fact that research about human beings can be called "social science" (as in psychology, anthropology, education, and similar disciplines), it is often difficult to give objective answers to research questions that address human subjects. This is particularly the case in arts education.

WHAT IS ARTS EDUCATION?

There are many confusions about the nature of arts education. Many of these are due to the early school experiences of today's adults who recall their own school days and assume that their own children are taught in the same way. But contemporary arts education has changed radically in recent years.

TYPES OF LEARNING

It is often falsely assumed that programs in arts education are entirely concerned with training young people to be musicians, painters and sculptors, actors and dancers. While today this may be the case with a tiny percentage of students - the highly talented who will become professional artists - it is not so for the vast majority.

Most students learn the arts in school in "the general program of studies": those elements of the curriculum thought essential for general learning and development. What are the purposes of the arts in such programs?

The literature about arts education clearly shows that contemporary arts education aims to improve all students' learning in three ways:

2

```
A          the intrinsic;
B          the extrinsic; and
C          the aesthetic.
```

These three types of learning overlap and intermingle
(Courtney, 1977a). For our purposes here, however, we
will deal with them separately. We should also note
that the modern focus on these aims is a change from
arts education in earlier times.

The arts provide intrinsic learning. They improve
qualities of the personality that assist learning as a
whole. These include: perception, awareness, concentration, uniqueness and flexibility of thought style,
expression, inventiveness and problem-solving, confidence, self-worth, and motivation. Learnings of this
type improve what is known as "learning to learn": the
students' general ability to learn, and their attitude
to learning. Students following the arts in the general
program of studies are likely to be better achievers
than those who do not have this opportunity (Courtney
and Park, 1980).

The arts improve extrinsic learning - learning in
non-arts subjects. The improvement of intrinsic learning, the students' motivation and ability in "learning
to learn," can assist learning in other subjects. There
is a generalized transfer of learning from the arts to
other areas (Courtney, 1982: 69-87). There have been
many research studies that indicate this. An example is
that visual arts can help to improve reading (Eisner,
1978).

The arts provide aesthetic learning in two ways.
First, the arts educate feeling. This can improve the
student's ability to make good judgments and choices in
the arts. Second, this transfers to all feeling - the
ability to discriminate, to make good judgments and,
thus, valued choices in all human activities. The
improvement of human feeling affects our emotions and
cognition in all spheres (Witkin, 1974).

Needless to say, these three aims of contemporary
arts education are not always achieved in a period of
educational change. There are some teachers in the
schools of Western post-industrial cultures who focus
their students' work upon the artistic skills of the
school orchestra, art exhibitions or the school play.
They are, however, a dying breed. There are others,
too, who for various reasons - inadequate training,

backward thinking, and the like - are not successful. Increasing numbers of arts teachers, however, aim at the intrinsic, extrinsic and/or aesthetic learnings of their students.

Researchers in arts education must be aware of the recent changes in the field. To commence inquiry with a series of out-dated assumptions is a recipe for disaster. It follows that those who engage in research about arts education should have practical knowledge of this specific field.

TYPES OF PROGRAM

Arts education programs vary in type, and every researcher should be aware of these differences. One of the first questions that an inquiry should address is: What type of program is this?

We have already seen that there is a difference between "general" and "specialized" programs. In the latter, adults training for a professional career in the arts, or school students within a pre-professional program (as in some High Schools for the Fine and the Performing Arts), are an elite group who need highly specialized programs. Specialized programs are required for particular populations - such as the physically or mentally handicapped. The vast majority of school arts programs, however, are not of this kind.

Another program difference is cultural. As one example, educational drama programs vary considerably between countries. In Britain, play with young children and improvisation thereafter are the ground for many programs; and theatrical performance is not a class but out-of-school activity with older students. Canada, Australia, and New Zealand are somewhat similar but there are exceptions: programs in British Columbia, for example, emphasize theatrical skill from Grade 9. In the United States, there is a major distinction between drama programs in elementary schools which are based on creative dramatics, and secondary programs which focus on theatre arts in the classroom. In Western Europe generally, programs that centered on spontaneous drama only began in the 1960's or 70's; where they do exist, many of them focus on drama as an agent of social and political change. In Tanzania and other black African countries, drama programs may be based on re-creating ritual activities which, only a generation ago, were

4

basic to the religious activities of the children's parents. In China, spontaneous drama as it is known in the West hardly exists; yet in some universities there are strong ESL programs based on both improvisation and role-playing taught by visiting Westerners.

There are also cultural differences of programs within countries - those of rural Prairie schools as compared with those in the great cities of America and Canada for example. What is possible in Dar-es-Salaam may not be in a school in the bush, and vice versa. And in today's multi-cultural cities, there can be program differences even between particular schools. In Toronto one class may have students from many language groups while another class in a nearby school may only contain Portuguese speakers. Both drama programs are different from a school I visited in Sydney, N.S.W., where the majority of students were recently immigrated Turkish adolescents and, as a result of their Moslem heritage, there was no way that the improvisational groups could include both boys and girls.

More obviously, there are program variations that result from national and local policies and practices, the attitudes of administrators, and the assumptions and practices of individual teachers.

These diversities indicate that researchers who have a weak background in the arts are disadvantaged. Then:

> The quick-silver nature of arts programs, the aesthetic subtleties in theatre, dance, film, music, poetry, visual arts and architecture, have been a source of embarrassment to many evaluators. They can be strengths. But it requires an evaluative approach responsive to the arts. In short, evaluating arts in education programs is not the same as evaluating spelling programs . . .It requires different readiness by the evaluators, different data, different sensitivities, and different interpretations (Stake, 1975: iv).

But because a task is difficult does not mean that it should not be done. This task is what the rest of this book addresses.

PART ONE

THEORY

Arts education requires a very different kind of preparedness and sensitivity of the researcher than is the case in many other instances. But in what way?

The arts are activities we value, some more and some less. Our values, however, are directly linked to our philosophy of life. In other words, our fundamental assumptions underlie the values we place on education as a whole and the components within it.

Our beliefs and assumptions about the nature and purpose of the arts, education, and arts education have a great effect upon our attitudes and judgments. Each of us starts from a particular perspective: how each of us values arts education is related to our assumptions as human beings.

Those who think the main purpose of education is cultural transmission say that there is an objective body of knowledge to be known. The aim of education is to transmit information and rules from the past; then students learn knowledge and values by imitating adults while teachers use reward and punishment. They stress literacy, numeracy, educational technology, behaviour modification or the mechanical rules of categorization. In arts education they can recommend the learning of arts skills that "rub off" on students from a master teacher, and an exposure to "great art" by which they learn "proper" ways to appreciate art.

But those who believe that what is natural to the child is good and that society unnaturally limits human freedom, have romantic assumptions. Thinkers such as Rousseau and A.S.Neill say that education should be so permissive as to allow the children's free expression. Their inner good should be permitted to grow and unfold naturally. Romantic arts educators emphasize emotional development. For Herbert Read, visual art should help to develop the child's natural potential while Peter Slade says that child drama is a natural and cathartic activity essential to education.

The philosophy of progressivists hinges on the work of John Dewey, particularly in the United States. Here people are organisms that learn by inter-action with the environment. When this belief is mixed with

7

the developmental psychology of Jean Piaget, the aim of education is to change students' patterns of thought by progressively solving problems. This to put an emphasis on cognitive and social behaviourism: the learner is goal-oriented and the active agent of change, not a mere recipient of instruction. In visual art education, says Dewey, teachers provide a stimulating environment but they do not intervene in a student's "learning by doing." The child's general creative abilities lead to integrative learning.

Holists, differently, vary in their assumptions from existentialism, gestalt, field theory and other philosophical approaches. Like Dewey, they think of the student as a self-activating whole, but most consider that learning is based on the intuitive knowledge of who one is - it commences from felt-knowledge. From inner feeling, the learner gives meaning to the world through mediation - the use of media. Thus the media of language and the arts are the basic educational tools.

These different philosophic approaches, as we can see, affect our sensitivity to arts education. Thus it is that researchers should ask of themselves:

* What are my assumptions about the arts and arts education?
* To what goals do these lead?
* How do they relate to the practice being examined?
* How do they affect my assessment and evaluation?

Part One provides an introductory background for such questions. Chapter 2 provides a history of inquiry by encapsulating the major points of view of each of the important philosophers in Western culture. Chapter 3 leads from pre-history to the end of the nineteenth century. Chapter 4 describes contemporary inquiry from Einstein to a range of perspectives that are used in research today. Chapter 5 looks at modern attitudes to knowledge and reason. This gives a background to the practical matters addressed in Part Two.

CHAPTER 2

THE HISTORY OF INQUIRY

"In whatever way the Deity should be
made known to you, and even if He
should reveal Himself to you: it is
you who must judge whether you are
permitted to believe in Him"
                                    - Kant

The researcher is a seeker of knowledge. "The
need to know" has been common to humanity since the
emergence of homo sapiens. Inquiry is a human activity.

Ways of knowing, however, have changed over human
history. The knowledge gained by Sir Isaac Newton had a
different character from the knowledge that was gained
by Pythagoras.

It is not that one of these great thinkers knew
more than the other, but that the kind of knowledge
they obtained was quite different.

Human ways of knowing hinge on "the world view"
(Pepper, 1942) of the culture in which the researcher
exists. It was possible to know certain things but not
others if the thinker was, say, a monk in the medieval
Church. This way of knowing differed, for example, from
what was known by a thinker in Paris at the time of the
French Revolution.

This is most obvious in the history of inquiry in
arts education. Here, the fundamental datum is people.
The human condition is the bedrock from which research
begins. But the nature of humanity, and its part in the
cosmos and the natural world, has been seen differently
over historic time. What people knew depended largely
on the intellectual notions of a particular society in
time. In other words, what the inquirer seeks will vary
with culture and history.

In order to understand modern research in arts
education, therefore, we need to understand the many
changes that have taken place in the past. Although
this is particularly the case with modern history, even
the most ancient research traditions linger today.

ANCIENT INQUIRY

In Western societies, the process of knowing has varied considerably over history. In some instances, forms of knowledge were in opposition: the medieval Church, for example, regarded the antique animistic beliefs of the people as evil and tried to root them out. But at the same time the Church also regarded the knowledge of Galileo as heresy.

Despite this, many different ways of knowing were incorporated in the Western intellectual tradition. For example, Aristotelian notions are part of contemporary thinking while animistic knowledge is incorporated in the thought of many rural people.

RESEARCH IN TRIBAL SOCIETIES

In pre-history, hunters and gatherers relied on the game and vegetation available to them. Humanity was tribal and identity was social.

Ancient beliefs had fundamentally the same kinds of structure as tribal and hunting people living today: Amerindians, aboriginals, Bushmen and others think the everyday world to be an illusion. "The other reality" consists of spirits that use "the clothing" of animals, birds, fish - all natural life, including people. Thus North American Indians are initiated through "a spirit quest" where a meeting with their guardian spirit gives them knowledge and "power."

Shamans (priests called "magicians," "sorcerers," "wizards" or "witch-doctors" - those who "doctor," or oppose, evil) are the expert seekers of knowledge in hunting tribes. Initiated in a trance ritual of death-and-resurrection, thereafter they use possession to seek out "power" from spirits. What they know are the skills of "research": how to make and control fire, how to seek "power," and so forth. The methods whereby they get knowledge by spiritual "power" are circumscribed by belief. They use the acquired knowledge, or "power," to assist the tribe by curing sickness or bringing rain, controlling the game, opposing evil and the like. Such knowledge is absolute. Any one who makes a mistake in a ritual might be killed. Viewed as researchers, shamans seek knowledge for practical ends: they work through the society's religious beliefs - the framework for action.

10

Central to the knowledge of a tribal people is the performance of the major ritual-myth. On Vancouver Island, this takes place nightly throughout the winter. The people (tribe) have an origin myth based on death-and-resurrection: a young hero is captured ("killed") by the Wolves; in their lair, he learns the secret of their "power" and brings this back to the people. The ritual re-enacts the myth with the initiate in the role of the mythical hero. Story (myth) and action (ritual) constitute unified knowledge.

Art as a discrete idea or category is not known. All of the arts are circumscribed by belief. They are created for the performance of the ritual-myths - the spiritual purposes as explicated by shamans and learned by the people through rituals. From a Western viewpoint a tribal inquiry in arts education is to research into absolute knowledge from a basis in action (Courtney, 1982, 1983, 1985b).

RESEARCH IN AGRICULTURAL CIVILIZATIONS

Over time, gods replaced spirits. With the rise of Mesopotamian civilization c.3,000 B.C., followed in sequence by those of Egypt, India, China and eventually of Central America, agriculture became the basis of a settled society. The emergence of king-priests having powerful armies permitted the storage of vast amounts of grain through the use of great numbers of labourers and slaves.

As each society became more settled and there was no need (as there was in tribal societies) for everyone to be occupied in securing food, many discrete roles and specializations developed. King-warriors became one class, priests another - except in ancient Egypt where the pharaoh was a king-god. Specialists in a variety of fields - carpenters, farmers, masons, scribes and the like - emerged, each with unique aspects of knowledge. The most esoteric, and the most powerful, were priests who were the seekers and possessors of secret religious knowledge.

Spirits in the ritual-myths of the early hunting tribes were suppressed but remained as chthonic beings - localized spirits with lesser powers. The farmers' new ritual-myths (also based on death-and-resurrection themes) became highly complex with various groups of gods having degrees of power.

11

Each god had specialized knowledge and abilities and the people mirrored this. The priest had two tasks. First, he maintained the inner secret knowledge of the gods: inner sanctuaries and private liturgies emerged. Second, he supervised and performed in the spectacular Festival Plays - great rituals of several days which nnually re-enacted the many complex myths that were believed to revivify life and the cosmos.

In this context, art was still conceived as part of the religious life. Various degrees of priests and acolytes were trained in the specialist knowledge or skill to create the drama, dance, music and decoration of the rituals. This knowledge, like the hunters', was absolute. But unlike the hunting rituals, it was not disseminated to the people; they were the audience who "witnessed" the ritual (in the Biblical sense). That is to say, the priestly class were the researchers or the inquirers: they sought secret knowledge on behalf of society.

RESEARCH IN THE CLASSICAL WORLD

The early Greeks inquired for knowledge that had the same structure and purpose as for all agricultural civilizations. But a series of invasions led to various city states which combined the ancient sacred farming traditions with those of the various invaders. There was as a result a whole series of changes in the nature of knowledge and the purpose of research.

Organized religion developed a variety of strains from the extreme of the "secret" priesthood of earlier civilizations to the ecstatic possession of ancient shamans. The worship of the "wild" Dionysos outcropped, giving knowledge once more to all worshippers and not merely priests; yet this knowledge remained secret to the cult. At the same time, the "mystery" religions emerged: they had more sophisticated beliefs than that of Dionysos yet they, too, provided knowledge that was highly secret to all who were initiated. In such cases, research was the maintenance of secret knowledge and the searching for new knowledge through ecstatic ritual action. Meanwhile Pythagoras had the abilities of a shaman, a musician, an astronomer, and a mathematician: for him, knowledge was not limited to categories but was "whole."

12

Using the earlier invention of writing, Homer was a seeker of knowledge who was able to write versions of mythology. The separation of myth from ritual affected views of knowledge. Homer's myths, declaimed aloud as models before the Athenians, were a knowledge base of the city in times of stress. They became the plots for Greek tragedy, performed by priests in the Theatre of Dionysos to an audience of the total citizenry. Here mythological knowledge, common to everyone, was acted by a select few: the specialist inquirer/dramatists who sought knowledge about the human condition within the cosmos through enactment.

The separation of myth from ritual through the invention of writing had another effect: the creation of science. Once myths were not enacted or transmitted orally but were written, they were examined objectively and found wanting. This led to some pre-Socratic thinkers who attempted to develop an objective science as the basis of knowledge.

"You can never step into the same river twice," said Heraclitus. Like other pre-Socratic philosophers, he emphasized change. But Socrates, Plato's master, was more concerned with self-presentation (human acting) as a way of knowing.

It was Plato, however, who gave the authority for objectivity and abstraction as valid knowledge. When he said that "Beauty" and similar abstractions existed separately from the mundane world, he opened the door to Aristotle and the emergence of scientific knowledge proper. For Aristotle the scientist, knowing came about through the logic of deduction and induction. Then life could, in abstraction, be separated into intellectual categories (physics, chemistry, biology, etc.) each of which could explain life within its frame of reference. Where earlier cultures saw life whole, Plato made it abstract and Aristotle divided it into parts.

Thus the Athenian world had a variety of models for the obtaining and securing of knowledge: shamanic ecstasy and Dionysian possession; illusion and change; self-presentation; the secret mysteries; myth and the rituals that enacted them now opposed by the rising discipline of history which relied on "facts" and not "lies"; the philosophic abstraction of Plato and the scientific objectivity of Aristotle; the Theatre of Dionysos with its Homeric plots, and so forth. These provided a plethora of models and, as a result, life in

13

Athens was culturally rich and diverse. But it was the model of the scientist as the researcher, abstract and objective, that was to have the greatest influence over the centuries (Courtney, 1986c).

MEDIEVAL RESEARCH

The medieval "world view" was, like all others, a system of truth-making. What was true, real and factual was a function of belief.

Expressed in a series of dominant metaphors, this belief was founded on the myth of the Christian epic as enacted in the Mass on the one hand and Mystery Cycles on the other. Life was meaningful because, no matter how difficult it was, it resulted from God's purposes. Faith and truth were one.

This truth was explicated by two groups. Priests were concerned with the truth of belief and disseminating this amongst the people.

Scholastics, however, were philosophers who discussed values, and scientists who addressed issues of the natural world. They developed the system known as "scholasticism": the guidelines and tools for scholarly inquiry and research and, thus, the frameworks within which social and spiritual truths could be discovered. Scholastic inquirers used reason as the major tool for knowing. Yet within the Church reason was an instrument of belief which had established the nature of God, the human soul, right conduct, and the relationship of God, nature and people. In other words, the Church provided the frameworks for social life and belief within which the scholastics researched (Courtney, 1974, Ch.7).

MODERN KNOWING

From the late fourteenth and fifteenth centuries, the Western intellectual tradition began to shift its mental foundations. This climaxed in the Renaissance and these changes have continued into the contemporary world.

EARLY SCIENTIFIC KNOWING

Two revolutionary events of the sixteenth century form the basis for modern ways of knowing.

14

First, Copernicus put forward the theory that the earth revolved around the sun, and this was verified by Galileo Galilei. The Catholic Church was well aware of the implications of this and opposed it vigorously.

Secondly there was a major change in the basis of truth. Until this time, religious faith and values had been the foundation for truth and, thus, of knowledge. While this continued to be the case for many people, a new basis was found in scientific objectivity - a view in strict contrast to that of the Church. Increasingly over time, science supplanted faith.

Galileo stated the new concept of truth: people and nature must be regarded as objects - that is, seen objectively; and inquiry must be based on verifiable methods - that is, empirically. In practice, therefore, researchers should restrict themselves to things and events that could be measured and quantified. All other aspects, particularly sensations, should be regarded as subjective and excluded from science. It is important to note that these scientific principles are upheld now by the most rigid empirical scientists.

Early in the seventeenth century, Francis Bacon proposed a clear procedure for empirical science: the inductive method. This was from the particular to the general: experiments were made, general conclusions were drawn from them, and these were then tested in further experiments. This inductive method provided a technology to achieve objective truth and knowledge. Importantly, also, it changed people's attitudes to existence: from adaptation to nature to control of it.

Bacon emphasized natural things instead of words. His great contribution to Western ideas was to apply science to daily life. He demonstrated that observation followed by experiment was the best method not only for science and technology but also for all aspects of life and living in the world. He said that the learner must rely on observation to discover facts, in addition to effective causes and results; whatever is discovered will then be true to nature, as well as providing the kind of knowledge that will be useful. In more recent times, this same method was the basis for the work of Mill, Watson, Pavlov, Skinner and other behavioural scientists.

Philosophically, there is no reason why induction as a method should not be favourable to arts education.

15

Yet this has not been the case. Inductive thinkers tend to go to extremes; they are liable to think that the arts are not "practical" - that is, they are not of use in the same way as engineering. This was particularly the case when induction was tied to extreme forms of Protestantism; thus the Puritans regarded the arts as mere diversions which drew devoted Christians away from the concrete and from "work." Bacon, however, was not so extreme: he commended the use of poetry in schools and, particularly, found great educational value in the "as if" of dramatic activities.

MECHANICAL INQUIRY

In the late seventeenth century it was Descartes and Newton who developed and codified these notions to such a degree that subsequent generations assumed they were truth. And it was Locke who brought similar laws to human society.

Descartes created the famous metaphor that all of life - the cosmos, nature and humanity - must be seen as a machine. He said:

> I do not recognize any difference
> between the machines that are made
> by craftsmen and the various bodies
> that nature alone composes.

From such a metaphor, Descartes could say that anything known must be known with certainty; there must be no doubt, no mere probability, for knowledge to exist. The way to achieve this, he said, was to use "the method of radical doubt": we must keep doubting until we get to that which cannot be doubted. As the only thing that doubt depends upon is the thought of doubt, then the fundamental truth upon which all other truths rely is his famous dictum, "I think, therefore I exist."

The implications of Descartes' machine metaphor echoed down the centuries. The specific machines used to illustrate the metaphor changed with mechanical inventions: in Victorian times it was the steam engine while today it can be the computer.

But whichever example was used, the metaphor was basic to later thought in three different ways. First, by identifying human existence with thinking, Descartes revived the ancient split between body and mind: he saw

16

mind as an immaterial substance set in the mechanical system of the body. This dualism had previously been part of Western intellectual traditions (particularly in the Jewish and Christian religions) but, now having Descartes' authority, it became a fundamental belief and assumption of many scientists even to the present day. Only in recent years has science come to see its limitations.

Second, Descartes thought of all natural life as mathematical. This meant that the way to seek for truth was through the abstract and the objective. Once such truth was discovered, it was totally verifiable.

Third, the machine metaphor implied that research was analytic. The way to inquire was to break reality down into small pieces - its constituent parts (like a machine) - and re-arrange those parts in their logical order. For Descartes, the whole was merely the sum of its parts: each distinct part should be verified in order to provide truth and knowledge. This idea, with its echoes of Aristotle, affected many later thinkers. Today elements of it can be found in educational ideas as different as Bloom's taxonomy, much of curriculum theory, and the application of Alexander Dean's work to theatre education.

It was through "the grand design" of Sir Isaac Newton that mechanical notions became fundamental to modern science. Newton's mathematical system explained the nature of the world as a machine within which he synthesized the previous notions of objective truth and knowledge. To this he added his own many inventions and discoveries. He created differential calculus to describe the motions of solids: within absolute time and space existed matter which was reducible to atoms; and physical phenomena were created through the motion of atoms - the result of fixed mathematical laws. Thus knowledge and truth were an integral part of a grand mechanical system. The inquirer sought to discover the events of cause-and-effect. Knowledge was completely objective without any interference from the observer.

PHILOSOPHIC INQUIRY

Modern philosophy, ushered in by Descartes in France, was given further impetus in the seventeenth century by Spinoza, Leibnitz and Locke.

Spinoza, a thorough-going determinist, accepted that people, nature and the universe operated like a machine through the irreversible laws of logic. But in saying that the human mind was an idea and also that its object was the body, he implied that thought was always "embodied" and, thus, knowledge was achieved by choice - a view that was to be expanded in the modern world as "tacit knowledge" (see pp.41-43).

Leibnitz, the founder of symbolic logic who made great contributions to statistics, probability, and conceived the notion of teaching machines, viewed time and space as illusions and matter as dynamic force the ultimate entities of which were "monads." Importantly for our purposes, Leibnitz distinguished reason from the intuitive which consisted of internal "feeling" experiences. This idea was to influence both Russell's theory of knowledge and some modern views of aesthetic thinking.

Descartes' question, "How do I know?" led to the British empiricism of Locke, and of Berkeley and Hume in the eighteenth century. John Locke described society and people through a system of natural laws that was as objective as those of his contemporary, Newton. Society (like the relation of matter and atoms) consisted of persons who were born with potentialities equal to all other people. At birth, the mind was "a clean slate" (a tabula rasa) upon which was written both all sensory experience and the effects of other people. Thus, like atoms, people were objects; their behaviour was the effect of the objective stimuli provided by society. The inquirer's job was to discover the knowledge that brought about the appropriate cause-and-effect relation (the truth of any human event) and arrange conditions so that people and society would behave appropriately.

George Berkeley accepted the empirical emphasis of Locke but said that neither abstract ideas nor matter existed. Rather, he attributed the perception of both to the Divine.

David Hume began to see the flaws in the current mechanical system of truth and knowledge. Nothing, he said, existed except perception and mental states; and statements of cause-and-effect were merely based on associations of sensory impressions - associations that were reinforced by habit or custom. This was virtually to deny objective knowledge:

18

The Humean point of view is important
because it affects all science, not
just theories of learning, perception,
and development, since the role of
the experimenter as observer is omni-
present (Campbell and Heller,
1980:30).

The implication in Hume's work was that objectivity was
to be replaced by the view that there was an underlying
similarity of human thought processes. But this did not
have a major effect upon science until the contemporary
era. Until the end of the nineteenth century at least,
the influence of Copernicus, Galileo, Bacon, Descartes,
Newton and Locke was pervasive in science.

These views also influenced arts education. In
seventeenth century Europe, little was achieved: the
inductive methods of Ratke and Comenius were based on
parts rather than wholes with an emphasis on "use" and
"practicality." Locke advocated learning based on the
sensations and reflection in order to form the habits
of mind that would lead to truth. But in advocating the
How of teaching rather than the What, Locke opened the
door (at least in theory) to possible indirect methods
(which might include art). He went further. For him,
the key to good teaching was the mutual relationship of
trust between teacher and student; and he asked that
learning should be as enjoyable and fruitful as games,
even approving of the use of plays and dancing. But he
also said that children should be treated as miniature
adults through discipline - thus opening another door
to those who emphasized discipline and ignored mutual
trust and enjoyment. The arts, being regarded as mere
pleasure, were not encouraged in seventeenth century
education because they were seen to have little to do
with truth and knowledge.

INQUIRY: THE ENLIGHTENMENT & KANT

In the eighteenth century, science codified and
assimilated the great change in knowledge and truth of
the last two hundred years. This was the time of "the
Enlightenment" - the period of Goldoni and Goldsmith,
Voltaire and Diderot, when the major purpose of art
was, as Pope said, "for instruction and delight." It
had to be "practical" with the strong moral basis of
sentimentality.

19

By 1750, Baumgarten separated "making" in general from the "aesthetic" for the first time. The result was the idea of a "disinterested interest" in art as the proper "aesthetic attitude" of a middle class audience. For the artist, there was a movement away from earlier issues of reality and illusion towards the notion of a "replica" of "la belle nature" - which involved a kind of prettification of the grimmer aspects of life. Still art remained essentially didactic and practical while, similarly, education was serious. Founded on the views of Comenius and Locke, it had to be of practical use.

But Kant's thinking was very different. His ideas altered. To begin with, he looked backwards to Leibnitz and others. Later, influenced by Hume and Rousseau, he was the foreunner of Heidegger and other contemporary thinkers.

Unlike mechanists, Kant says that science must deal with things as they appear (phenomena) but must also provide an understanding of them. His question becomes, How can these two elements be synthesized to bring truth and knowledge? His answer is to proceed by both simultaneously: it is reason that provides the synthesis and makes up our ontological and existential reality. In this way, Kant in effect says that there are three levels of reality that lie along a continuum between the poles of unity and multiplicity: (1) the everyday world of the phenomena in experience which we transform; (2) the world of scientific knowledge which is achieved by analysis; and (3) the ideal (Plato's abstract) world.

Kant assumes that there are moral laws which all persons must obey - "the categorical imperative." We know what is right by intuition, which is the pure form of practical reason. Practical reason has priority over pure reason - a major difference from mechanists - and the two are synthesized by "the aesthetic." It does so through "feeling" (approval) which transforms our human perceptions into human judgments. Both play and art are modes of the aesthetic: it is the feeling act of mind which provides a kind of knowledge and truth. When Kant unites practical and abstract knowledge, he gives to aesthetic knowing a priority over practical reason.

But Kant goes even further. In saying that play and the aesthetic provide knowledge, he re-introduces the dramatic "as if" into Western ideas. Although this had been the view of Heraclitus, Xenophanes and other pre-Socratics, Plato and Aristotle had subordinated it to pure reason. Paradoxically, Kant appears to do the same yet he also says that play "fictions" in fact do create knowledge. Abstract ideals are what he calls "heuristic fictions" - fictions that lead us to find meaning. In other words, knowledge is discovered within the play of appearances.

The importance of Kant to our theme lies in the fact that he frees art from any necessary association with usefulness, or pleasure, or morality which it had possessed before him. Art exists in its own right as a mode of the aesthetic: although it deals with the play of appearances, it provides knowledge and truth. Human experience of art (and so its educational purpose) has the result of increased mental alertness, a heightened vitality, and a clarity of feeling above the ordinary. Kant emphasizes moral education which can be achieved only if children engage in free, practical activities in the manner of Rousseau. But the implication is that play and the arts are forms through which we achieve knowledge and truth.

It is no wonder that his views had little effect upon the mechanists who were then dominating science. His ideas had to wait two centuries before they became highly influential in science.

ROMANTIC & 19TH CENTURY INQUIRY

From the end of the eighteenth century, a diverse range of views about knowledge infused Western thought.

Romantic thinkers disagreed fundamentally with a machine metaphor but, while they influenced all social, political and aesthetic ideas, they had little effect upon pure science. Denis Diderot adopted a biological view of life and the universe: he considered that the everyday world and personality were mere illusions - thus linking the notions of Heraclitus with Bergson and Pirandello in the twentieth century. At the same time Jean-Jacques Rousseau, who was more influential, said that what was natural was true: knowledge was obtained through free and spontaneous activity - an idea with a profound influence upon both art and education, but not on science.

Romanticism relied on wholes rather than parts. To inquire was to seek synthesis, an idea that lay at

21

the root of its predilection for "the dialectic." This method was fundamental to Hegel who thought truth to be cyclic: thesis + antithesis = synthesis, which becomes the thesis once more.

The dialectic was intended to change the duality of existing science into the notion of the whole, but it actually achieved a triad. This triangularity only partially changed the machine-like binary approach and could not quite capture the notion of the whole. With Heraclitus, Hegel said that all is change. Yet he also believed in one whole, unified and absolute truth - "the Absolute," which consisted of the relationships between the triad of the dialectic. Hegel's influence was considerable on philosophers in the nineteenth and early twentieth centuries - Bradley, Royce, Dilthey, Croce, Alexander, Whitehead, Dewey and, of course, Marx and Engels - but he had less effect upon the physical sciences.

Determinists during the nineteenth century made significant contributions to knowledge: economic and historical with Marx, evolutionary with Darwin, and psychological with Freud. Karl Marx used materialism to produce the dialectic of socio-economic history: thus, capitalists + the proletariat = a classless society. Economic production determines the social structure of a society; material existence determines the ideas of the people. These ideas were the basis of "scientific socialism" of later Marxists and communists. But it was perhaps Marx's greatest contribution to Western social science that our sense of reality is the relationship between persons as social beings and physical nature: namely, a unity of thought and action, a specific form and content of consciousness, and a specific form of cooperation (social form).

The determinism of Charles Darwin was a kind of evolutionary naturalism. From antiquity it had been assumed that there was a chain of nature that had a fixed hierarchy. But evolution showed that life and the universe was an ever-changing system with forms moving from simplicity to complexity. This has much support from contemporary findings in D.N.A., although Darwin's idea of "the survival of the fittest" is questioned.

For Sigmund Freud, the unconscious determined our conscious thought. All symbolic activities - in dreams, play and art - represented repressed desires and wishes through manifest content (what we perceive) and latent

22

content (our repressed desire). Art was a healthy form of expression of what otherwise might be unhealthy.

Despite this variety of views as to the nature of knowledge and truth, mechanism was still the foundation of science. It had also become the commonplace way to understand life. Industrialism infused all aspects of society: cause-and-effect, quantity more than quality, measurement, and the purely practical use of ideas and things were uppermost in most people's minds. Induction was the nub of Utilitarianism - "the greatest happiness of the greatest number" - and in its most rigid form, as with John Stuart Mill, it was basic to behavioural scientists.

CONCLUSION

Before we move to modern inquiry, it is important to re-state that these previous views of research were culture-bound. To a medieval Christian, as well as to a Victorian mechanical scientist, a shaman believing in a spiritual reality was "a savage heathen." Yet all three were genuine seekers of knowledge.

The human quest for truth is always framed by the metaphors of mind.

CHAPTER 3

CONTEMPORARY FORMS OF INQUIRY

"However deeply the player is
committed to his role, he is
never wholly unaware that his
character is unreal"
- Sartre

The mechanical system was under attack by the end of the nineteenth century, but it was still believed to be basically correct. With the great discoveries at the beginning of this century, the belief in mechanism as the only way of knowing began to crumble.

THE EFFECT OF RELATIVITY

Contemporary physics has replaced the metaphor of the machine with the key idea of relativity - the unity of space and time. In essence, this shows that truth is not absolute. Nor is knowledge. They are, rather, only perspectives on space-time.

CONTEMPORARY SCIENTIFIC INQUIRY

When in 1905 Albert Einstein published his first three papers, not only the world of physics was turned upside down. His theory of relativity changed the way the human species looked at itself, the natural world and the cosmos. This led to a new attitude to inquiry and research.

The inter-dependence of space and time, and the curvature of space-time, the unity of gravitation and inertia, quantum theory and so forth, had vast effects upon subsequent thought of all types. Fundamentally it meant that matter is not made of solid particles but can be explained in two ways:

1   as particles occupying a very small space; or
2   as waves spread out over vast regions of space.

Thus the causal is not the only way to find truth; nor has matter any intrinsic qualities independent of its environment or of the means used to observe it.

To mechanists, knowledge was certainty. But in contemporary science, predictions of future events can only be made in terms of statistics - as probabilities. The probabilities of matter are not probabilities about objects; they are more like probabilities about events, about inter-actions. Estimation through the theory of probability is a way of knowing. Inquiry, that is to say, is a matter of highly informed guessing. Certainty has been replaced by guessing or "pretending to know."

Mechanical science had said that the whole was the sum of its parts. But contemporary physics shows that the whole determines the behaviour of its parts. Objectivity, verifiability, and value-free research have been shown to be a myth founded on belief, in much the same way as the myths of the ancient and medieval worlds.

Importantly for quantum mechanics and all other kinds of research, Werner Heisenberg formulated the Uncertainty (or Indeterminacy) Principle in 1927. This stated that a particle may be said (a) to have position (in space); or (b) to have velocity (in time); but (c) it cannot WITH ACCURACY be said to have both. For the researcher, this has significant implications:

1   Two observers can make different observations of the same event and both can be right. Truth, in other words, is relative to the researcher's point of view.
2   Two ways of acting may be equally valid. Just as there is no one way to learn to ride a bicycle, there is more than one appropriate way to seek and discover knowledge.
3   Our mental structures decide how we order any kinds of experience. As mental structures depend upon society, so do our constructions of reality (Berger and Luckman, 1966).

To simplify: inquiry in arts education depends upon the researcher's perspective; this may differ from someone else's viewpoint; and both views are largely socially constructed.

THE INFORMATION METAPHOR

Some contemporary scientists have replaced the machine metaphor with the metaphor of information. From the work of Claude Shannon, "information" has been seen as a scientific term: it is an active agent that gives shape and pattern to life; it specifies the character of living forms; and it helps to determine, by means of special codes, the patterns of human thought. Thus Watson and Crick showed that the double helix of D.N.A. was an information system.

The theories of information and probability show that in the mind of the actor (speaker) there are many possibilities for action. Which of these will be chosen is uncertain.

Human choice becomes a fundamental fact. Once an actor chooses what and how to act (the particular message), one possibility has become actual while others have been excluded. Uncertainty has been resolved: the witness (listener) is no longer uncertain of the action and no action (message) can be considered in isolation but must be understood as a relationship in the context of all other actions.

From this perspective, human action is a code. It works within a statistical framework as both created and stored information. It restricts the choices of the actor by introducing redundancy: some possibilities are more likely than others.

But for action to be a successful code, it must retain a maximum amount of freedom, a wide variety of possible enactments, so that it can be both meaningful and intelligible. Without a code, action would be of no use. It would be so free as to be chaos: it would have no intelligibility, no protection against error, and no complexity. Obversely, if there is too much structure then creativity is cramped, patterns become resistant to change, entropy takes charge and everything falls into disorder.

THE DRAMATIC METAPHOR

Underlying much of contemporary research in both science and social science is the dramatic metaphor: knowledge is secured by creating fictions with which we interact. Einstein's revolution can be seen as the triumph of the postulate (a logical fiction) over the axiom, or fixed law (Muller, 1943). Einstein talked of the realities "created by modern physics." These are the "scientific fictions" of Hans Vaihinger where, as Niels Bohr said, we are both actors and spectators at the same time. This scientific use of the metaphor has been followed by social scientists and, particularly, researchers in education. They have shown that "models" as "aesthetic fictions" are significant to inquiry.

When McLuhan says, "The medium is the message," he shows that in today's world of "electric media" (the extensions of the electric circuitry of the brain) it is not What but How a message is transmitted that has importance. Thus we dramatize knowledge not merely by taking roles; we "put on" the media themselves. We then exist in a play world, and:

> Real play, like the whodunit, throws the stress on process rather than product, giving the audience the chance of being a maker rather than a mere consumer (McLuhan and Fiore, 1969: 173).

This is to return to the flux of change like Heraclitus and modern biologists. Thus Henri Bergson says that the thrusting force behind life is a creative compulsion of endless duration, a view echoed by the General Systems Theory of biologist von Bertalanffy.

In a similar way, Alfred Korzybski and general semanticists acknowledge that life is a process, a real dynamic which we attempt to capture in "maps." But "the map is not the territory" and within any inquiry we are engaged in "a play within a play."

One of the most influential notions in the social science of today is "the dramaturgical perspective" of Kenneth Burke. He says that knowledge IS action. When people inter-relate they do so "as if" they are actors playing roles and, thus, there is an act, an agent who employs an agency, a scene, and a purpose. We dramatize our relationship to others and the world; then we not only create symbols but create a symbolic world that is our perspective on the physical one.

For Burke, life IS a drama: action is structured behaviour in terms of the symbolic "as if." This leads to choice, conflict and cooperation in communication between people. Society is a drama where our "as if" actions (as social symbols) are the crucial events. For Berger and Luckman subjective processes are objectified so that an interpersonal construct occurs and this, say Lyman and Scott, means that life is theatre while the

28

social world is inherently dramatic. Like Shakespeare, this is to go further than, "All the world's a stage," to, "We are such things as dreams are made on."

This is also to rely on the view of personality of G.H.Mead: life is a monodrama between the elusive "I" and the visible "Me." Mental life, on this view, requires the skills of a playwright, a director, an actor, a cast of players, an audience and a critic which, unified in the mind, can be distinguished as concepts for analytic purposes. In terms of inquiry, Erving Goffman says that it is only through the drama of social life that we can uncover one another's mental life.

In anthropology, a similar view is maintained by Victor W.Turner who shows that ritual is the main way in which a society maintains social order. The rituals of importance in any society he terms "social dramas" which discharge tensions in the social system. They are "rites of passage" which, as in the classic instance of initiation, have three stages:

1   separation from a previous group;
2   liminality - the transition state; and
3   incorporation into the new group.

The liminal state is the crux of all ritual: through Being "as if," it produces reflexivity which heals a social breach by enacting it. That is, as inquirers we should not only seek social knowledge by dramatization but we must also acknowledge that society inevitably creates meaning in the same way.

The essential lesson of contemporary science and social science is that there are more ways than one of seeking knowledge. Today there is a plurality of ways of knowing. Inquiry is essentially a perspective on people, things or events.

Nor is there one metaphor with which inquiry can work. Models, information and drama have been used as metaphors to successfully inquire into life, nature and the cosmos, and there have been a variety of others.

Perhaps the most important thing the contemporary researcher must remember is that we cannot produce an absolute answer to a question or find only one rule for action.

PHILOSOPHIC PERSPECTIVES

Contemporary philosophy accepts that there is a plurality of methods of inquiry. In fact, philosophy amplifies this scientific view in a variety of ways: according to pragmatism, phenomenology, existentialism, idealism, structuralism, realism and analysis. We will examine these in turn.

PRAGMATISM

The American philosophers, C.S.Peirce, William James and John Dewey are pragmatists, each asking of an idea "What consequences will it have on our lives?" not "Is it true?" And each of these thinkers is concerned most with process.

John Dewey has the greatest influence on social scientific research, specifically in education and art, and in two ways. First, as a process philosopher, he emphasizes that inquiry is:

1   Contextual - problems are placed in their context - their immediate setting.
2   Relative - the data and solutions of research are relative; there are no final solutions in human science.
3   Concrete - all issues are rooted in actuality.
4   Genetic - researchers ask, How did it get that way?
5   Continuous - researchers look for continuities rather than differences.
6   Whole - inquiry should emphasize the whole not the parts.

These principles have affected inquiry into education, particularly in curriculum theory and arts and aesthetic education. In Dewey's view, personal considerations will affect all knowing, and knowing is based on activity - which has profoundly influenced North American ideas.

Seemingly in contrast, in social science Dewey was influenced by G.H.Mead's "social behaviourism," and he developed the experimental method of research. He said that when a problematic situation results in doubt the following scientific procedures should take place: the problem is observed, defined and analyzed; hypotheses are made that bear on the problem; these are analyzed and feasible solutions are chosen; and then finally we

30

test these solutions empirically or inductively and draw conclusions. The resulting "truth" satisfies not only the individual but also society. This method of inquiry has particularly influenced educational psychology.

We should note that Dewey's principles and method have been used in a variety of ways by modern research in aesthetic education (Madeja, 1977-81).

PHENOMENOLOGY

Phenomenologists are concerned with what happens from moment to moment - the "essence," or What-ness. They deal with how we are aware of phenomena and how consciousness deals with them. Kant said that we both sense phenomena and try to understand them in the use of abstraction; and that we unify them through the mode of the aesthetic. Brentano, however, unifies them by saying that consciousness is "intentional": even in sensation, mind refers to an object - it is "consciousness OF."

It was Edmund Husserl who founded contemporary phenomenology: the science of the descriptive analysis of subjective phenomena. Phenomena are the ways things present themselves to mind; and they are the data of consciousness. From Husserl's viewpoint, the inquirer seeks knowledge of consciousness through three methods:

1   the phenomenological reduction - the immediate data only are described, while all explanations are "bracketed out" (i.e., held in suspension);
2   the eidetic reduction - the "essence" is always abstracted from the data; and
3   the comparative analysis - between the object that is presented in consciousness and the object of knowledge (e.g., between the sound we hear and the "essence" of sound).

The knowledge that results consists of three elements:

A   the Self found within the individual's stream of consciousness (the basis of truth);
B   the acts and intentions of the Self;
C   the referents (objects) of consciousness.

For Husserl, therefore, the researcher must distinguish these three elements in a phenomenological description of events. But the observer's knowledge is also related to three levels of the Self:

31

* the mask, or social role;
* the Self, or person who acknowledges the social role;
* "the unobserved observer" who apprehends both the mask and the Self.

Inter-subjectivity, on the other hand, is achieved through empathy: the researcher must see things not as a private world but "from the other's point of view" - essentially a dramatic act. Knowledge of the Self and the world (including others) is what we "live through." Husserl's phenomenology is a method of inquiry that must attempt to capture the on-going present.

Contemporary phenomenological research assumes that human reality is negotiated reality, and that what is negotiated is meaning. It is liable to use a variety of methodologies - by direct observation, unstructured interviewing, theme analysis, interpretations of structure and so forth.

EXISTENTIALISM

Existentialists do not deal with "essence" but existence. They focus on human life that ends in death - "that-ness." When mechanism was at its height in the early nineteenth century, Kierkegaard saw subjectivity as both truth and reality. Nietzsche, somewhat later, rejected cause-and-effect, objectivity, and the logic of dialectic. He gave "the aesthetic world" priority over abstraction which was mere fiction - a person was both player and plaything. These notions have been developed by contemporary existentialists but in very different ways.

Martin Heidegger deals with the immediate, living experience and not explanations (abstractions) of it. He describes self-presentation as truth and knowledge. This provides him with a particular stance for inquiry. We are authentic yet self-conscious when we choose: we are "thrown into the world" without choice; we both dread our finitude and yet have to Be. This anxiety becomes a "nothingness" because it has no intentionality. Thus authentic despair occurs when we realize that our life aims towards death, an experience we must face on our own. Then we decide what we are to become.

From this position, Heidegger in his later work develops the notion of Being as a cosmic game. It is

32

play that grounds Being - its nature derives from play. Time and space play in, and with, human beings while God plays with people and the world. This "world play" is the basis of Being - truth is the play of dis-closure. Heidegger says that we are played by play, an idea close to Wittgenstein's "language games."

That knowledge and truth are revealed through and in human play is developed by two of Heidegger's pupils, Fink and Gadamer. Eugen Fink says that play appearance is more "real" than actuality because, as a mode of knowing, it comes closer to Being than phenomena. Play provides an "enhanced reality" which enables the whole to appear but on a limited scale (much like a hologram). That is, for Heidegger and Fink play is spontaneous and irrational and cosmic: it reveals knowledge "whole" and not as a false abstraction or in part truths.

The foci of any existential human inquiry are play and art for Hans-Georg Gadamer. Play is not subjective, nor is it aesthetic consciousness. Rather, it exists for itself medially. Playing is self-representation. Play and art are media that exist in and of themselves: the players and artists "no longer exist, but only what of theirs is played." Art totally transforms the world: "It is a part of the essential process of representation and is an essential part of play as play."

Thus Heidegger, Fink and Gadamer and others who follow Kant, regard inquiry as an examination of Being. They consider that knowledge is best revealed through self-presentation in play and art. "Play fictions," or "aesthetic fictions," are ways human beings operate in all aspects of existence, not merely science.

The actor (whether in life, science or art) uses his performance to create meaning in the "out there." What he acts IS his symbol system. But as an observer, he views the performance AS a symbol. He can only fully understand the meanings created from his own frame of reference; others do so from their frame. The two views are not necessarily the same; they are complementary. To mutually understand any event, two persons must agree on their complementary languages or communication cannot take place. That is the essence of working in the "as if." Thus dialogue occurs.

The great Jewish philosopher, Martin Buber, gave to existential research his concept of dialogue - as opposed to dialectic. When young in Vienna, he found the world of the theatre which lies at the heart of his "I and Thou" relationship. The theatre gives a heightened illustration of the human drama which is dialogic: it transforms the abyss between people so that each can "become" the other. This is the mutual relation of "I and Thou" where each person confirms the other as of value, and sees things from the other's point of view. In contrast is the "I and It" relation where each person uses others as an object and does not value them. The essence of inquiry is a dramatic relation of two people.

As part of this dramatic perspective, Buber asks for a particular stance from the researcher: a genuine human inquiry lies in the mutual respect for others, the fostering of each person's sense of freedom, the sharing of visions and hopes with one's fellow human beings. A researcher who is evaluating an arts program from the perspective of Buber would initially ask the following questions:

* What is the dialogic relation of teacher/student?
* Do they or do they not "acknowledge" each other?
* Does the teacher deny the arbitrary "will to educate" and see things from the student's point of view?
* Does the relationship encourage the capacity for growth and potentiality in the context of human friendship?

Different yet again, the French existentialists Marcel, Camus and Sartre are artists and philosophers. Each addresses the issue of aesthetic fiction. Jean-Paul Sartre, like Husserl but unlike Kant, says that the appearance of concrete phenomena constitutes reality. Most importantly, he shows that imagination brings about the affective-cognitive synthesis: we cannot manage our perception or emotion of the external world; as a result imagination creates an object with which we can deal. Thus Sartre can say that imagining is "a species of knowledge," and what is imagined is externalized in action. But the actions of life, play and aesthetic fictions are analogues of what we imagine.

From Sartre's perspective, any inquiry that begins from observing human action infers that each actor is transforming the actual in terms of the imaginative. We can observe the child at play, the adult using social roles, or the player taking characters on the stage; but we must distinguish between three types of emotion in the human actor:

1   sham emotions - those of self-conscious acting;
2   unreflective emotions - those that are involuntary
    and are believed; and
3   reflective emotion - the recognition of one's
    no-thingness.

        Each existentialist is different and has a unique
attitude to inquiry. What is common to them is their
stance, their focus on human existence as a moment that
is between birth and death.

IDEALISM

        Contemporary idealism, based on Plato, Kant, Hegel
and Bradley, is also influential in contemporary inquiry
into the arts.

        Aesthetic play in consciousness is intuition: "the
creative imagination" of Benedetto Croce. It is formed
of feelings and images; this we then express externally
unified by feeling. Thus our expression has a knowledge-
value apart from its embodiment in a work of art.

        Like Kant, Ernst Cassirer says inquiry is always
about form - "symbolic forms": the formal structures
which, as symbols, underpin life, science and art. Also
deeply concerned with form is Suzanne K.Langer for whom
art works are "forms of feeling." These are specifically
not representations or imitations but "virtual" objects
- abstractions whose content is "semblance." "Forms of
feeling" do not express actual feelings but ideas of
feeling. With Cassirer and Langer, therefore, methods of
inquiry are similiar to those of structuralists.

        An idealist allied to pragmatism is Harold Rugg, a
friend of Dewey, who says that there is an aesthetic way
of inquiry based on imagining. This is exercised in the
creative act of "the transliminal mind": situated midway
between the conscious and unconscious, this is where
thinking mingles feeling (in discovery) and logic (in
verification). Knowing is therefore primarily "an inside
identification with the object" and only secondarily "an
outside and measured evaluation of it." Similarly, any
inquiry is first from inside the situation (qualitative)
and only thereafter quantitative.

        Robert W.Witkin combines Langer's aesthetics with
Piaget's psychology into a rich sociology of aesthetic
knowledge. Based on a research project with thousands of

school students, his inquiry shows that the inner world of sensations and feelings is the source for a person's motivation and enthusiastic response to life. There are two poles of behaviour: my sensing of the feeling within me ("subject-response"); and my actions which change the world ("object-response"). Play and aesthetic fictions exemplify the intelligence of feeling based on subject-reflexive action. Most importantly, Witkin describes four "whole" mental structures which are related to the Piagetian structures of scientific thought:

> Pre-Adolescence:
>   semblances (addition), contrasts (subtraction), harmonies (multiplication), and discords (division).
> Adolescence gives increases in complexity:
>   identities, polarities, syntheses, dialectics.

These structures of aesthetic thought have also been the basis of other research studies (e.g., Courtney, 1985a).

STRUCTURALISM

Structuralism has been inherent in many types of inquiry since the turn of the century. However, it is only since the 1950's that it has had a major impact on research in psychology (Piaget), anthropology (Lévi-Strauss), criticism (Barthes), philosophy (Foucault), psychoanalysis (Lacan) and many others.

The structural method of inquiry is to search for the underlying structures of an activity - e.g., the economic as with Marx, the unconscious as with Freud, or the "deep structure" of language as with Chomsky. Thus Lévi-Strauss even tries to reveal the various underlying structures of the human mind as manifested in language, cooking, dress, manners, art, myth and various social expressions. Similarly, Barthes roams over a very broad spectrum of literacy and other interests. Like earlier mechanists, he breaks the whole down into constituent parts before "reconstructing" it so that it becomes "a fiction." The structural method allows us to observe actions and behaviour and then infer the inner mental structures of the actors.

Allied to structuralism is semiotics. Semioticians investigate "languages" (including arts "languages") through signs. They distinguish between:

1   the signifier - the sign, or form, that signifies
    something; and
2   the signified - the meaning of the sign.

This methodology can be used for inquiry in two ways:
General Semiotics (philosophic questions), and Specific
Semiotics (analyses of particular languages). Elsewhere
I have examined the semiotics of aesthetic knowing and
learning (Courtney, 1985a).

    Post-structuralists, reacting against the binary
methods of some structuralists and the restrictions of
semiotics, make their inquiry much wider. Thus Jacques
Derrida works with similarities rather than oppositions
and puts forward a new form of logic:

*   it is not that A is opposed to B;
*   rather, B is the negative of A; B is both added to
    A, and replaces A;
*   it is not the opposite to A: it is a "supplement"
    (both an addition and a substitute) to A.

This type of logic, and the semantics of A-J. Greimas,
allows Floyd Merrell to put forward a method of inquiry
based on the metaphor as fundamental to all thought.

REALISM & ANALYSIS

    The British school of philosophical realism turned
to analysis as a method of inquiry. Major thinkers such
as G.E.Moore, Bertrand Russell and Ludwig Wittgenstein
focused their inquiries upon epistemology and provided
many insights into ways of knowing. We will discuss this
in the next chapter.

CONCLUSION

    The twentieth century change in methods of inquiry
has been radical: from one appropriate methodology, the
mechanical, to virtually as many methods as there are
questions. Today in our quest for knowledge, once the
research question has been established, a second quest
must be undertaken to find the method that will address
the question appropriately.

    This specifically does not mean that quantitative
research must be abandoned. Indeed there are questions
that need to be addressed in terms of measurement. Where

37

the greatest care must be taken, however, is with what is known as "experimental research" - the application of Newtonian mechanics to human settings. There have been many studies that have inappropriately used this method.

Any inquiry is culture-dependent, as we have seen. This means it should initially establish:

1   the refinement of the question;
2   its function:
    a   the value function: the purpose of the inquiry;
    b   the aesthetic function: the organizational symmetry of theory and model development;
    c   the editorial function: specification of the parameters, limitations, etc.;
    d   the methodological function.

These are not a hierarchy: each will inform the other. At best, the assumptions of the researcher will marry with the context of the inquiry.

In the final analysis, we must chose a method that depends upon the type of knowledge we seek about arts education in THIS specific context. This issue will be addressed in the next chapter.

CHAPTER 4

CONTEMPORARY KNOWLEDGE & REASON

"Neither observation nor reason is an authority. Intellectual intuition and imagination are most important, but they are not reliable: they may show us things very clearly, and yet they may mislead us. They are indispensable as the main sources of our theories; but most of our theories are false anyway. The most important function of observation and reasoning, and even of intuition and imagination, is to help us in the critical examination of those bold conjectures which are the means by which we probe into the unknown."

                    - Sir Karl Popper

In arts education inquiries, what are the best ways to know? Which ways to approach issues will not lead us into error? For irrefutability, what reasons can we use, and when? To which methods can we turn, in case of doubt, as the last court of appeal?

No such ideal sources exist, as Popper has shown. There are no perfect rules or laws of these kinds.

All ways of working and all sources of knowledge are liable to lead us into error at times. If we appeal to "pure" knowledge, untainted knowledge, we reveal a metaphysical assumption that may be unconscious in us - that knowledge derives from the highest authority (most probably, God). As Popper goes on to show, "questions of origin or purity should not be confused with those of validity or truth." That is, metaphysics should not be confused with epistemology.

The researcher in arts education is concerned to uncover what has happened, what is happening, or what might happen. By engaging in educational inquiry, we become "a seeker of knowledge" and "want to know." But the methods used to discover knowledge are all subject to error. Nor can their results be absolute "truth." At best they provide valid perspectives on what exists. The issue, therefore, becomes: which can be the valid method to discover knowledge in this particular and unique instance?

KNOWLEDGE

But what is "knowledge"? Until we have a general idea of what we mean by this word we cannot adequately discuss methodology.

Contemporary attitudes vary but there are two fundamental ways of looking at knowledge: (1) by kind; and (2) by type. In neither case are their categories discrete; all exist simultaneously. The categories are theoretic: they are intellectual and abstract "maps" of an experiential process.

1   KNOWLEDGE BY KIND

A   Knowledge IN
B   Knowledge ABOUT

While we exist within the experience of events we secure knowledge IN the activity (e.g., as we sing or dance, etc.). We gain this as we live in the temporal process that continues, the present, the "now." We are not always conscious of gaining such knowledge; yet paradoxically not all of such knowledge is unconscious.

Knowledge ABOUT, in contrast, is gained when we study the temporal process from outside as it were (e.g., as we talk about singing, dancing, etc.) We are not part of the activity from which we gain knowledge but we are usually (if not always) conscious that we are doing so.

Making such a distinction between knowledge by kind is not to separate body and mind; it is not to fall into the dualistic trap. Rather, these kinds of knowledge co-exist. The emphasis upon one rather than the other is according to two simultaneous events: the kind of activity; and the focus of our attention.

This way of looking at knowledge derives mainly from twentieth century philosophers, particularly two who, although they had considerable disagreements, had some resemblances in their thought. Bertrand Russell made an important epistemological distinction between: (1) "knowledge by acquaintance," or direct empirical evidence; and (2) "knowledge by description," or to think and talk about direct experience. John Dewey made a distinction between knowledge gained through action and that gained through deliberation. These kinds of distinction are similar to those of Knowing IN and Knowing ABOUT.

Depending upon which kind of knowledge is used, definitions will differ. Knowledge ABOUT is likely to use the type of definition, as in dictionaries, which describes the unique qualities of things and actions (called "denotative" or "intentional" definition).

Knowledge IN, however, is likely to use a more personal understanding of things and actions, such as examples ("connotative" or "extensional" definition). Thus definitions within Knowledge ABOUT are likely to describe differences and distinctions while those of Knowledge IN are likely to provide examples of things or actions.

2   KNOWLEDGE BY TYPE

        A   Tacit knowledge
        B   Explicit knowledge
        C   Practical knowledge

        Tacit knowledge, called "personal knowledge" by Michael Polanyi (1964), is primarily unconscious and intuitive. But explicit knowledge is that which we know consciously. This is the type of knowledge that many teachers have often (falsely) assumed to be the only kind of knowledge.

        We usually obtain explicit knowledge when we talk or write about experience. It is, therefore, closely linked to (though not necessarily the same as) Knowing ABOUT. It is usually expressed in language, written or spoken.

        Tacit knowledge, in contrast, is implicit. It cannot be formulated explicitly in words but it is the foundation of our assumptions, beliefs and hunches. It underlies virtually all the actions and decisions that we make in everyday life. Moreover, it is the basis of all explicit knowledge. Each of us, as Polanyi says, knows more than we can tell.

We learn such tacit knowledge without the use of conscious cognitive processes: we create an unconscious "map" of how things and events work. If we attempt to express tacit knowledge in words, it changes. Language uses a different kind of "map" from the "map" of tacit knowing. Tacit knowledge is retained over a long time; in contrast, explicit knowledge is relatively fragile (Allen and Reber, 1980).

Importantly for our purposes, tacit knowledge has a metaphorical structure. But metaphors are not merely characteristic of language. They are fundamental to all "languages" including those of the arts. Moreover, they are the generic base of all thinking, specifically that which is tacit. Tacit knowledge is metaphorical in that it always involves two notions: we understand one thing in terms of another, through their similarities. Thus, in language, the metaphor "the roses in her cheeks" is to understand "her cheeks" in terms of "roses."

We can illustrate the metaphoric nature of tacit knowledge from the bodily metaphor. From birth, we are tacitly aware of the world through our body: concepts of "near" and "far" are formed in relation to our body. It is through the notion of the body that we come to know space and this underlies all subsequent spatial knowledge. Marshall McLuhan can develop this concept to say that the pen is the extension of the hand and the wheel is the extension of the foot. Tacit knowledge is structured around many such metaphors.

This structure brings a double dynamic. In tacit knowing, we know two things not one. Unconsciously our attention is focused alternately on two things: the metaphorical aspects of what we know. That is, when we know tacitly there is not a one-to-one relation between our knowing and what we know. Rather, we know the two sides of the metaphor, seemingly, simultaneously; in fact, our attention oscillates between the two sides in a dynamic.

How can we characterize this double dynamic? It is based on the initial structure of human thought: of similarity/differentiation, or whole/part. From this initial structure, we come tacitly to know two things:

1   the actual world (the "really real"); and
2   "the play world" (the not "really real"), often called "the aesthetic world" or "the fictional world."

The actual world is as we all understand it - a table is a table and a picture is a picture. However, "the play world" is a mental representation of the actual world: created through imagining, it consists of what the actual world MEANS TO US. It is based upon feeling but it has cognitive and affective aspects and works metaphorically. With increasing complexity it becomes symbolic of the "really real."

This "double" structure of tacit thinking and knowing is closely allied to the way in which artists work. They express an "aesthetic world" through their artistic medium. An art work is a representation of the actual world as the artist understands it. The arts act in a fictionalized world: they are metaphors - that is, representations of the actual - and they operate within symbolic forms and processes.

For researchers in arts education, knowledge by type is highly significant for two reasons:

1   Tacit knowledge underlies all other knowledge of human beings.
2   The tacit dimension, when symbolically expressed through a medium, is the domain of the arts in particular.

But what is practical knowledge? This, the third type of knowing, is also important for research in arts education.

Practical knowledge is the knowledge-base for the reasoning that we use in the everyday world. It is not just common-sense: it is common-sense used very well. It has two dimensions: the tacit and the explicit. It provides us with "Know-how."

Practical knowledge is how we work in order to make our judgments and our choices. Good artists have a good practical knowledge of art, good teachers have a good practical knowledge of teaching and good gardeners have a good practical knowledge of gardening. It may be that the content of practical knowledge differs from person to person, but its structure is similar amongst all people.

Practical knowledge is strongly bonded to each person. Yet it can be changed. Thus when teachers meet a method of teaching they have not known before, they may try it out; if it does not work for them, they may

43

reject it and retain their former practical knowledge; but if it does work, they may alter their practical knowledge accordingly.

Researchers in arts education require:

1   the practical knowledge to conduct research;
2   to understand the practical knowledge of learners, artists, and all of those engaged in arts education (teachers, administrators, etc.)

But if practical knowledge is the knowledge-base for practical reasoning, how do we reason? and specifically how do we reason when we are engaged in arts education inquiry and research?

REASON

Reasons are the ways we make judgments. Modern views of reasoning are wider and more inclusive than was previously believed to be the case.

STYLES OF REASON

When we conduct research in the modern world we should be aware of the different styles of reason that are available to us.

Aristotle said that there were two main kinds of reason: deductive and inductive. For many centuries, these were regarded as the only "objective" reasons - the only ones that provided "truth."

Deductive reason is from the general to the particular, as with the logic of the classical syllogism:

> All men are mortal.
> Socrates is a man.
> Therefore, Socrates is mortal.

"All men are mortal" is a generalization (a hypothesis of a general kind) from which many particulars can be deduced. This is characteristically used in science. Thus Darwin, in his theory of evolution, counted up myriads of instances and, from these particulars, he supported his generalizations.

Induction is from the particular to the general (see p.15 above). It is characteristically used in mathematics. From one theorem we assume all similar cases follow: for example, the angles of all triangles add up to 180 degrees.

Earlier in this century, Ludwig Wittgenstein gave a different perspective on reason. David Best, whom we will follow here, has reinterpreted this view in terms of arts education by asking, "How do we know that this Chinese dance is good?" His answer is through "criteria in context" - we use specific criteria (from reasons) within a specific context.

The criteria we use when judging a particular Chinese dance can be based on:

1   deductive;
2   inductive; or
3   interpretive or moral reasons.

Justifying, commending or explaining direct experiences by moral reasons (which derive from a person's tacit assumptions) is common in everyday life. Interpretive reasons convey the salient features of many patterns of behaviour in relation to their moral character. We must use these reasons within the context of Chinese dancing as a whole to make a valid judgment about it. If we know nothing of the context of Chinese dance, whatever criteria we use will be to little purpose.

The use of "criteria in context" is the modern way of reasoning not only about art but also about all forms of human operation, specifically in education. It is the way that teachers make judgments about students, that administrators make judgments about programs, and that researchers make judgments about their data.

SUBSTANTIATION

Substantiation is a way of stating that "this is the case." It is a way of ensuring that what is known is as near to the truth as human methods will allow. There are two familiar forms of substantiation:

A   the empirical; and
B   the logical.

The empirical is given by "going and seeing": by observing, gathering information, and investigating. This can occur in two basic ways: inductively, so that the many observed instances lead to a generalization; or deductively, so that the generalization is assumed to be supported by the gathered data. Empirical methods are best at answering questions that begin, "How many?" They usually make explanations in terms of cause-and-effect and quantity.

Logical substantiation is different. Although it must match observation, it is based on logic. It makes explanations in terms of "criteria in context." Human beings have reasons for what they do; such reasons may be implicit or explicit to them; either may be inferred by observers.

Both the empirical and the logical can be viewed as "objective": they provide substantiation through what actually occurs or exists. However, the logical is not empirical: it requires no additional investigation or information.

Unfortunately there is a popular (but false) view that only the empirical is objective. Indeed, empirical investigations and causal explanations are of use in some situations but not in others. They cannot, for example, capture the notion of chess as a game: a move in chess is given its reason from the context of the total positions of the pieces on the board, together with all of the conventions of the game - a matter for logic.

Likewise many issues in human affairs must take into account the total circumstances. In many cases, to explain human action is to explain a relationship - the relationship of the contextual factors, or the dynamics of the exchange. A researcher can only tackle issues of these kinds through logic and not through causes.

Whereas in mechanical inquiry classical logic was thought to produce "truth" because it was "objective," contemporary logic is thought to be objective but not to produce universal and absolute laws. This is because one thinker may use one criterion while a second may use another. One may come to a different conclusion from another. Thus I may judge this dance to be good while you may not. You may hang one picture on your wall. I may hang another.

This does not make our judgments invalid. Rather, they are relatively valid: one is just as valid as the other if it is based on good reasons. This is seen most obviously when two good critics mutually disagree as to the aesthetic value of a work of art.

Yet there are not infinite possibilities of valid judgments. In order to be valid, any judgment must be logical. That is, it must be based upon "criteria in context." If two valid judgments result in different inferences then, simply, we should accept that this is the case. As Wittgenstein said, "that's that!"

BEING RIGHT & BEING WRONG

When we inquire into arts education, how do we know when we are "right" or "wrong"?

As we have seen, neither the knowledge we use nor the knowledge we acquire will involve absolute "truth." As Sir Karl Popper has said, knowledge evolves through a series of conjectures and refutations, of tentative solutions to problems, checked by substantiation. What matters, Popper points out, is whether the conjectures are right.

If a conjecture holds up despite all the various objections we can raise against it, then we have no reason to suppose that it is not right. In Popper's terms, being right is quite good enough. In the final analysis, whether the issue is theoretic or practical, a researcher should be right.

How do we know if this is the case? Much depends upon the fundamental question addressed by the inquiry. If it is a quantitative question such as, "How many students in this music program can do X?" then a normal and straightforward experimental procedure, correctly carried out, will usually satisfy most experts that the results are right. But most inquiries in arts education do not ask such questions.

Inquiry in arts education most often addresses qualitative issues where the results are not so hard-and-fast as those of measurement studies. In these cases, conjectures must be criticizable. Qualitative questions raise critical arguments - negative arguments that require refuting by the researcher. Conjectures from which critical questions can be refuted must, in

47

common-sense, be based upon fact. If empirical issues
are raised, they should be answered empirically; and
rational issues should be answered through reason. In
common-sense, if the researcher can adequately answer
critical questions then the findings of the study are
likely to be right.

In the quest for knowledge about arts education
the prime issue, says Popper, is, "How can we hope to
detect and eliminate error?" Then we must ask whether
the conjecture or assertion agrees with the facts. We
achieve this by examining and testing the conjecture or
assertion, subjecting it to critical arguments - all
kinds of arguments. If it stands up to this test then,
in common-sense terms, it will be right.

THE EFFECTS ON ARTS EDUCATION

How can we ensure that our research or inquiry
into arts education can be substantiated?

While empirical evidence might be used to answer
some research questions in arts education, reasons must
be used in other instances. In still further instances,
both may be used. It is part of the practical knowledge
of the researcher to decide which is appropriate in a
particular case.

There is a logical relation between meaning and
the medium in which it is expressed. In the case of
language, the meaning of a word or phrase is given by
the various sentences in which it is used. They derive
their meaning from the whole activity of language of
which they are a part.

The same is true of meaning in arts education.
Meaning requires a context. This specifically applies
to the arts. In all of music, drama, dance or visual
arts education, meaning is given by the context of the
action, or the complex of actions, of which it is a
part. A particular dance movement (e.g., a gesture) may
have different meanings in its different contexts; in
effect, it IS different actions.

Assessments of arts students, or evaluations of
arts programs, may well differ from a similar type of
judgment or assessment made from a similar framework
but in a different context. For example, I can make a
judgment or assessment in two different contexts - say,

in Toronto and Dar-es-Salaam. Because the contexts are
not the same, my inferences and conclusions may well be
different.

Differences in judgment are particularly related
to interpretive and moral reasons. Not everyone can see
the same thing in a work of art - I can interpret it
one way and you may interpret it another - and much may
be due to our tacit assumptions. In the same way, the
facts about an action (in drama, say, or dance) depend
upon how it is seen; that is, it depends upon one's
tacit attitude towards it. In terms of inquiry, we must
take into account not just an isolated physical event
but, implicitly, wide factors - like the circumstances
in which it occurred, our knowledge of the person(s)
concerned, and so forth.

In this sense, research in arts education is tied
to a whole cultural tradition and the life of a whole
society. The imposition of a colonial program and its
values upon a subjugated culture, or of middle-class
assumptions on working-class students, can result from
a failure to use the logic of criteria in contexts.

Further, individual differences of sensitivity
and understanding can affect research in aesthetics and
arts education. They alter the possibility of seeing
and responding to what takes place in arts classrooms.
To fully appreciate arts education, the researcher must
have developed the capacity to imaginatively grasp and
respond to complex interactions specifically in the
arts, in teaching, in learning, and in education as a
whole.

We all have our own frames. The many individual
differences only make sense against a background of
objective meanings. But objectivity is relative to
cultural, not individual, differences. The meaning of
arts education for which we seek depends on a social
conception given by our mutual dramatic life.

In other words, when we engage in research and
inquiry in arts education we should:

1   have the practical knowledge to do it well;
2   understand the practical knowledge of all
       engaged in the enterprise; and
3   examine the effect of social contexts upon
       criteria and meaning.

CONCLUSION

The modern researcher of arts education seeks knowledge, achieves this through reasoning, and then substantiates it. He or she attempts to understand the meaning of particular kinds of events and explain them to others. To do so requires practical knowledge that includes ways of working with knowledge, reason and critical questions so that the meaning of the inquiry is understood by others. As Sir Karl Popper says, this is not necessarily easy:

> With each step forward, with each problem we solve, we not only discover new and unsolved problems, but we also discover that where we believed that we were standing on firm and safe ground, all things are, in truth, insecure and in a state of flux (Miller, 1985).

PART TWO

PRACTICE

Part One examined the philosophic history of both
research and inquiry in arts education to the present
day, and specifically in terms of the knowledge we seek
and the reasoning we use. This background is part of
the preparedness and sensitivity of the researcher.

It is not the total necessary background. There
are instances when an inquiry may require expertise of
other kinds: in one or more of the arts, in curriculum
praxis, and in an aspect of psychology, sociology or
social anthropology. The inquirer must draw on these
and other fields as the needs arise. But basic to any
inquiry are the important assumptions it contains: the
total perspective of what is being attempted.

Part Two looks at practical decisions and some
examples of arts education projects. Where in Part One
we examined Why, now we turn to How and What.

One thing is certain: if the reader is wanting a
simple answer to such questions as, "What do I do now?"
and, "How do I do it?" it will not be found in the
following pages. We no longer live in a world governed
by mechanistic laws where X was thought to cause Y, or
if A was done then B would result. When we research in
the arts we are dealing with complex human issues. They
cannot be dealt with in simplistic ways.

As we have seen in Part One, our own particular
perspective will not only be part of the research, it
will to a large extent affect our practice. During any
inquiry, and at any stage, "What do I do now?" might be
answered in one way by a phenomenologist but another by
a pragmatist. So much hinges upon our own philosophic
assumptions, and the nature of the particular task in
hand, that it is impossible to give a precise answer
to, "What do I do now?"

Those who research into arts education today are
particular people who inquire into particular problems.
They must transform the theory of Part One into their
own specific practice. This theory/practice interface
is known as "praxis." Praxis is an elusive and slippery
matter which, as it relies on human decisions in human
contexts, resists precise definition. In arts education
good results depend upon:

51

1   The nature and context of the problematic.
2   The sensitivity, practical knowledge and skill of
     the inquirer.
3   The relation of the inquirer to the problematic.

Under these circumstances, human decisions at each step
of the inquiry will close some doors and open others.
To discuss practical procedure, therefore, is to talk
of possibilities.

     As a result, Part Two will provide a display of
possibilities. Chapter 5 will look at possible research
frameworks in arts education, including a display of
methodologies. Chapter 6 will examine ways to approach
a thesis. Chapter 7 will provide background for program
evaluation and give some examples. Chapter 8 will then
indicate other research styles, also with examples.

CHAPTER 5

RESEARCH FRAMEWORKS IN ARTS EDUCATION

"We know next to nothing about virtually
everything. It is not necessary to know
the origin of the universe; it is necessary to want to know. Civilization
depends not on any particular knowledqe,
but on the disposition to crave
knowledge"

                  - George F.Will

In arts education, the quest to know What? Why?
and How? is ongoing in the twentieth century. There are
various frameworks for this inquiry. This chapter will
address the types of inquiry and a display of methods.

TYPES OF INQUIRY

We can distinguish various types of contemporary
inquiry into arts education as follows:

1   STYLE

           A   Teacher materials
           B   Scholarship
           C   Research

Teacher materials, which include classroom texts,
"how to do it" books, audio-visual aids, and the like,
have increased rapidly in recent years. Allied to these
are in-service workshops of a practical nature. Looked
at as forms of inquiry, these can be at a low level,
although there are exceptions as when they are directed
by a master teacher.

Scholarship and research can be distinguished in
many, if not all, instances. Research is to address a
specific issue in order to discover what is the case.
Scholarship is to use learning and wisdom to reveal
significant aspects of an issue which may well be wider
than that addressed by research. But in some instances
it is impossible to decide that an inquiry is one or
the other.

The situation varies between different countries. Scholarship in Britain has reached a high level but research in arts education mainly consists of a small number of Schools Council projects, a few M.A. theses and fewer dissertations. This is paralleled by the work in Australia.

In North America, things are somewhat different. Theses and dissertations are increasing rapidly. In the 1960's and 70's there were various research projects funded by governments, foundations, etc., but recent projects have not kept pace. Scholarship, which earlier in the century was given impetus by Dewey's educational work, is now more often focused in allied fields - creativity, aesthetics, etc.

2   CONTENT

       A   General -   aesthetic education,
                        integrated arts, etc
       B   Specific - music, visual arts,
                        drama, dance, etc.

While there are always some inquiries about the general arts in schools, there is little on integration - although there are some studies about the place of the arts in the education of young children. From a basis in Dewey, there have been studies in aesthetic education (a general field that is based on "aesthetic awareness") in the United States but little elsewhere.

Subject matters differ radically in scholarship and research. Materials are greatest in visual arts and music. In comparison, there is little in drama and even less in dance. We should note, however, that there are isolated exceptions focused on individual scholars and researchers in various places in the world.

3   FRAMEWORK

       A   Of Fine Arts disciplines
       B   Of Education and its
                  sub-disciplines
       C   Of other disciplines

We have seen that research is culture-dependent but this is nowhere more obvious than in the arts. The particular intellectual frameworks of institutions, of funding and cultural agencies, often determine the lens that is used. For example, a university tends to place a specific art in a category; then the sub-culture of that category may determine what is an "appropriate" research framework and what is not.

This is best illustrated in a particular example, namely: drama/theatre studies in Canadian universities. Some instances are:

* Alberta at Edmonton - drama is one of Arts and Sciences;
* Victoria B.C., and Calgary - drama is in both Fine Arts and Education;
* Toronto - drama is one of the Humanities;
* McGill - drama is in The Department of English;
* both Montreal and the Ontario Institute for Studies in Education - drama is in Education.

On the surface, this may appear to be simply a matter of nomenclature but, as Korzybski said, often "the name creates the fact." Thus when drama is placed in one of the above categories, thesis methodologies may be as follows:

* in Arts, Humanities, or English - literary, historical (M.A., Ph.D.);
* in Fine Arts - practical interpretation (M.F.A.);
* in Education - curriculum, applied psychology, etc. (M.Ed., M.A., Ed.D., Ph.D.).

Each category has its own frame, not permitting others. This is further complicated when an individual student researches an aspect of drama in a still different academic category.

For example, a drama student who is in one of the categories listed above may study the relationship of educational drama to ritual; but ritual may be viewed as part of Anthropology which might be sited in Arts and Sciences, or Social Sciences, or Sciences - and in each case the permissible academic frameworks may be different.

In contrast, research projects funded by agencies (governments, foundations, industry, etc.) may not be limited to academic categories. However, they tend to have their own intellectual frameworks which lead to specific guidelines. Agencies are normally precise as to the question to be addressed, and the researcher has to find the methodology that is both appropriate and efficient.

Thesis students should particularly note that, if they intend to become professional researchers in arts education, they will have to enlarge their repertoire of research skills from the one methodology of their dissertation to agency frameworks.

DISPLAY OF METHODOLOGIES

"Which research method shall I use?"

This ubiquitous question from those who are about to embark on a thesis is not a simple one. Nor is it easy in other types of inquiry. As we have seen, much will depend upon the research question to be addressed. It is worth repeating, moreover, that empiricism is not the only valid method of inquiry. For some research questions it is inappropriate while for others it is appropriate.

The following display of methodologies is not exhaustive but indicates the main frameworks:

STYLES OF RESEARCH AS A WHOLE

Many textbooks on research as a whole begin by dividing the topic into four areas:

1   philosophical
2   historical
3   descriptive
4   experimental.

In contemporary arts education, the field is dominated by experimental work there is an increasing number of descriptive studies. There are some historical studies and a smattering of philosophical inquiries.

STYLES OF EDUCATIONAL RESEARCH

Research in education per se has widened considerably in recent years (Courtney, 1982: 192-97). Back in 1963, the standard view (e.g., Borg and Gall, 1963) was that there were two types: (1) the descriptive; and (2) the experimental, called "causal," as follows:

1   DESCRIPTIVE METHODS attempt to describe rather
         than explain phenomena in the following styles:
*   Survey Research.
         Instruments of data collection (e.g., question-
         naires, interviews) are linked to statistics for
         analysis. A general example is the Gallup Poll;
         an arts education instance is McLeod (1978).
*   Observational Research.
         Direct observation is followed by analysis by
         specific criteria. An arts education instance is
         McGregor, et. al. (1977).
*   Historical Research.
         The systematic location, evaluation and synthesis
         of historical evidence leads to conclusions about
         past events (e.g., McCaslin, 1971).

2   CAUSAL METHODS attempt to deduce (or induce)
         causes for phenomena in the following styles:
*   Causal-Comparative Research.
         Causes for behaviour are deduced by comparing
         subjects in whom this pattern is present with
         similar subjects in whom it is absent (e.g,
         Anastasi and Foley, 1944).
*   Correlation Research.
         Relationships are discovered or clarified through
         correlation coefficients (a statistical tool), as
         with Huntsmann (1979).
*   Experimental Research.
         This is the most rigorous causal method, the
         other two often being part of this design. It
         manipulates one variable, observing its effect on
         another item (e.g., Lazier, Sutton-Smith and
         Zahn, 1971).

         It is almost a quarter of a century since this
classification was regarded as standard. It has been
continuously revised to meet changing needs, one of the
most valuable up-dates being that of Connelly et alia
(1980) whom we will follow here. Today the following
types of educational research are possible:

1   BY KIND

*   Empirical - experimental and causal, as above.
*   Historical - as above.
*   Analytical - phenomena are analyzed through
                  criteria, frameworks, classifications, or
                  categories.
*   Naturalistic/Descriptive   (and   Narrative)   -
                  phenomena are observed and described as

                           57

they exist or operate in a variety of possible ways, usually followed by some element of analysis; qualitative rather than quantitative.

* Philosophical -
  a   historical, analytic or descriptive of theory;
  b   generation of theory;
  c   application of theory to phenomena with analysis.

2   BY FUNCTION

* Confirmative - verification of previous research.
* Exploratory - empirical investigation of a hypo-thetical relationship between two or more variables.
* Theory/Concept Development - development of such notions related to phenomena.
* New Perspective - a previously researched issue examined from a different perspective/discipline.
* Program Evaluation (see Chapter 6) -
  a   diagnostic provides initial information to set activities in motion;
  b   formative provides ongoing information as to the functioning of the program(s);
  c   summative provides information as to what the program has achieved.

3   BY METHOD

* Statistical - usually supports empirical studies.
* Criterion referenced - criteria in context, usually supports rational and qualitative studies.
* Survey - data are collected from a sample (tests, questionnaires and/or interviews) and sets of scores are examined.
* Case study - uses one sample of a unit (person/event/school, etc.); can be experimental or naturalistic (Cottle, 1977).
* Field study - phenomena are observed with/without a framework; a sample greater than one.
* Content analysis - analysis by criterion referen-ced themes within data.
* Educational criticism - descriptive method based on the attitude of the critic of art (Eisner, 1979) and, by extrapolation, of other types of critics.

*   Model building - development of theoretic models,
        often tested empirically (Horning, 1982).
*   Participant observation - observations by resear-
        cher of an activity in which s/he is a
        participant (Spradley, 1980).
*   Phenomenology - study of direct experience (Valle
        and King, 1978); variations include:
        Personal Record/Diary - participant experience
        recorded in the present tense (data)
        revealing of an educational issue.
        Dialogic - participant observation by researcher
        with one other: e.g., counsellor/client,
        visual arts master-teacher/student, etc.
        (Andrade, in: Peavey, 1985: 259-267).
        Critical incident - direct observation of/
        participation in significant "critical
        incident" that meets specific criteria
        (Fivers, 1980).
*   Context analysis - use of systems theory to dis-
        cover basic structural units within data
        and then reintegrate them into a whole
        (Santen, in: Peavey, 1985: 245-57).
*   Grounded theory - non-hypothesized collection of
        data from interviews and then content
        analysis to "ground" an "emergent" theory
        (Glaser and Strauss, 1967).

OTHER AVAILABLE STYLES

        The above styles are those commonly available to
the arts education researcher. Depending upon the kind
of inquiry and the nature of the research question,
however, other quite different methodological styles
might be used for arts education studies. For example:

*   Scholarly methods of various kinds can be useful
        for philosophic, historical, analytic, theoretic
        and conceptual studies, or aspects of studies.
*   In some program evaluations, experiential methods
        may be useful. Some clients wish their arts
        teachers to be part of an experiential process as
        well as receiving a written report. In such a
        case, the outcomes of the research study are two:
        1   a diagnostic/formative/summative style of
                evaluation by the researcher, usually but
                not necessarily in writing;
        2   improvement of arts teachers in program
                planning/implementation and/or teaching
                skills and strategies.

"Multivariate" research (Kerlinger, 1979) is an interesting methodology. Based on advances in computer data analysis and statistical theory, it combines quantitative procedures with qualitative data. Specifically it can sensitize the researcher to various individual differences.

CONCLUSION

Unfortunately, arts researchers have not always led in developing new styles of inquiry. This may be due, at least in part, to the continual need to justify the place of the arts in schools and to persuade some parents and taxpayers that these are not "frills." As a result, studies have often been framed in conservative styles in order to demonstrate the respectability of arts education. This simple faith in the effectiveness of research to accomplish what is, in fact, a matter of political persuasion is touching but usually quite ineffective.

Another factor may be the academic situation of thesis supervisors. If they are in a Department of Art, Music, Drama or Dance, or a small Faculty of Education, they may have a heavy work-load of undergraduate teaching, with little time for graduate instruction and less for helping thesis students. Then they may lack good expertise in supervisory skills and find themselves at a disadvantage with other committee members. In these circumstances, supervisors should concentrate their efforts in improving their background and skills in research.

A further factor is the lack of externally funded research in arts education. This leads to a lack of good research experience throughout the field. It is my experience that it can be a great struggle, with much expenditure of energy, to try to secure support for arts education research - particularly when the present educational climate hinges on platitudes like "back to the basics," accountability, and so forth - and the result is often unsuccessful.

There is great need for universities, as well as governments, foundations and external agencies to give support for inquiry and research in arts education. Without this, research will remain inadequate and new methodologies will not emerge.

60

CHAPTER 6

THE THESIS

"Art is that which is the most
real, the most austere school of
logic, and the last judgment"
- Proust

This chapter will describe various aspects of the preparation of a thesis in arts education.

It will outline the main problems to be faced by those commencing a thesis. It will not, however, give examples of theses or attempt to provide an exhaustive analysis of problems. Not only do institutions differ in their requirements but arts education dissertations, as we have seen, can occur in a variety of disciplines which also differ in their expectations of theses. Thus the discussion presented here can be regarded as merely an introduction to the key issues in order to assist those who are just beginning.

PREPARATION

The preparation of their thesis is the single most important element in the background of researchers in arts education today. How one prepares oneself, the work methods learned, the skills of observation and inter-action together with the practical knowledge that is acquired, give a unique stamp to the new inquirer's later career. He or she should also remember that, in many cases, a researcher is known throughout the field by the quality of his or her dissertation.

Individual institutions and disciplines usually have their own specific ways to prepare both theses and dissertations. It is obvious (although it must be said) that candidates for higher degrees should follow the procedures approved by their discipline and university. Thus I have omitted questions of writing style and the preparation of references and the like which can be the subject of considerable variation.

The following represents recommended ways whereby candidates should THINK about arts education theses and dissertations.

TOPIC

Theses topics vary by value, depth and content as follows.

VALUE

A thesis topic should address a problematic that is of concern to the student. A thesis and a graduate degree represent a sizeable portion of a life; thus it should be of significance to it.

Social science is not the cold, objective and distanced study that is the hoped-for image of certain mechanistic thinkers. It is a human science - a value-laden and value-directed activity. The topic should be important to the field: it should address a problem of significance. It should focus on an issue so that the candidate can work on ways to achieve understanding about it and expertise with it. The criteria for value in the field are improving art(s), improving education, and improving arts education.

Theses also provide basic materials for the many subsequent scholars and researchers in arts education. They will benefit most if the problem addressed is a significant one.

DEPTH

A topic should strike a balance between depth and limitations.

It should be capable of being pursued in depth so that the final thesis will have something significant to say. There will, of course, be a difference in depth according to whether the final product will be at the level of a master's thesis or a doctoral dissertation. In either case the focus of the study, the nature of the question it addresses, and the quality of the work should be of the depth to earn a graduate degree.

To limit the framework whereby a question can be examined in depth is a necessary condition of calibre research. It provides a focus that leads to clarity and precision of study. In most cases of high quality work, the limitations give an intellectual lens whereby the candidate can focus on the key issue.

62

CONTENT

It is best if the topic is of great concern to the candidate. It should also be linked to an issue about which some knowledge already exists. This will prevent the candidate from working in a vacuum. It will give him or her a good place to begin, and provide a useful check as the work proceeds. The final results should enhance previous knowledge by verifying, extending and/or refining it.

A thesis topic, together with the way in which it is addressed, should not replicate that of an existing thesis or dissertation. It is the candidate's duty to check (through "Dissertation Abstracts," etc.) that this is not the case.

THE THESIS QUESTION

After initially considering the topic that is to be examined, the thesis question should be prepared.

IMPORTANCE OF THE QUESTION

This is a vital step. It has been said: "Get the question right and everything else falls into place." It gives a coherence first to the Proposal, and second to the writing of the thesis.

An appropriate question certainly provides the necessary focus - a precise "cut" through the many of the complex issues that can complicate a candidate's thinking. I recommend that a copy of the question is prepared on card and sits on a candidate's desk to keep his or her mind on the issue at hand.

This does not mean that a thesis question cannot be changed at a later date. It often can, although in exceptional circumstances. It should be avoided where possible but, if it should occur, then the new question becomes just as important to the candidate as the old.

THE NATURE OF THE QUESTION

The question should encapsulate the problem to be addressed and the manner of doing so.

Education questions, in order to encapsulate the problem, normally incorporate two nominals (X and Y), such as, "What is the effect of X on Y?" More concrete examples might be:

A   What light can Piagetian developmental psychology (X) shed upon a Grade 4 Music program in the Province of Ontario (Y)?
B   Does creative dramatics (X) improve the self-concept of Grade 2 students (Y)?

Both of the above are good examples of how to BEGIN to prepare a thesis question.

The first (A) needs further refining before it is satisfactory: thus which specific aspects of both (a) Piagetian psychology, and (b) the music program, will be addressed, and how?

The second (B) is much more explicit and "clean." It is nearer to a genuine thesis question because it implies the methodology to be used. It indicates cause-and-effect as a relationship - and that implies the use of a quantitative method of some kind. Questions that begin, "How many . . . ?" or are framed as, "Does X affect Y?" imply empirical and causal methodologies.

RISK TAKING

Arts education candidates do tend to take risks - probably more so than many graduate students in other fields. This may be because people in the arts are high risk-takers, or that they enjoy both creative problem identification and solving - or all of these.

The kinds of risks they are liable to take are two:

A   Those of content.
     Many express the desire to address some existential question of cosmic import, or X's that, on the surface at least, appear to have little rational connection to Y's.

B   Those of methodology.
     Many state their wish to use some kind of new methodology, often from a related discipline (such as holistic psychology or an aspect of Eastern mysticism), which may or may not have stood the test of time.

64

In my view, candidates should be informed in such cases of the risks they are considering. It is not that risk-taking is a bad thing: indeed, inquiry in the arts and education is in real need of new approaches and perspectives. But students should be informed of the realities of the thesis examination: examiners tend to like students to be "objective" which can, in certain circumstances, merely mean "conservative." However, if candidates must take risks, I advise taking one risk, not two. I often repeat something that Brian Way once said about writing plays: "You can use either a new content or a new form. Use both, and the audience will likely walk out!" And I add: "And in thesis writing, if you have to take one risk - if you do - you had better do so brilliantly."

THE COMMITTEE

Universities have different ways of establishing committees, the time at which they have to be formed, the number of committee members, and other procedures. However, the following may be helpful:

1   The candidate and the supervisor refine the topic and question together.

2   The candidate writes the Proposal, checks it with the supervisor, and has it approved by the committee.

3   If an oral examination will be necessary, rehearsals are wise. It is good practice for the candidate to face questions from the committee when presenting the Proposal and, in addition, when each complete draft is ready.

4   Candidates should remember that all committee members (and all examiners) have different work habits, forms of expertise, personalities and expression. Where candidates can choose the supervisor and the committee members (and I regard this, personally, as essential) then they should choose:

*   a supervisor with expertise in the topic, and with whom they can work well and easily; and
*   committee members who can cooperate well together and whose individual expertise will be helpful in the work involved.

65

THE PROPOSAL

The purpose of the Proposal is to demonstrate to the thesis committee that: (a) the candidate is well prepared for the proposed study; and (b) has all the necessary skills to do so. The candidate should realize that these are qualities with which the committee will be concerned.

Procedures and styles will vary with the specific institution, but the following may be helpful:

1   The first draft is prepared under the supervisor, and the final draft is approved by the committee meeting as a whole.

2   Proposals will likely include:
*   Introduction, that may state
     -    the problematic in general terms
     -    what is being studied and why
     -    the candidate's background preparation in relation to the study
*   The Thesis Question
     -    the question stated
     -    sub-questions stated
     -    hypotheses (if any)
     -    limitations
*   Background to the Problematic, in terms of
     -    education as a whole
     -    arts education
     -    the conceptual framework(s) of the study
     -    background to the literature of the two aspects of the study (X and Y, as above)
*   Design of the Study
     -    redefinition of the thesis question in operational terms (how, in the study, it is to be addressed)
     -    methodology outlined which may include
              kind of data to be collected
              how it will be collected
              how it will be treated
     -    task analysis of expected steps
     -    possible time schedule
*   Expected Significance of the Study
     -    how it will add to present knowledge
              in education
              in arts education
*   Conclusion
*   References
     -    provisional book list

66

3   Length.
        There is no perfect length for a Proposal.
I have received some of 7 pages, some of 70. But if it
is longer than 20-24 pages (typed, double-spaced) the
candidate should have very good reasons for its length.

                     WRITING THE THESIS

        By the time the writing stage is reached, the
candidate should have a very good idea of what is and
is not expected. This can be achieved by discussion
with the committee and other candidates, as well as by
reading previous theses, including those of different
institutions.

        It is best to keep the supervisor informed of
progress at all times. Supervisors differ as to whether
they wish to view drafts by chapters or by the whole.
How far committee members wish to be informed of the
candidate's progress should be negotiated with them at
the beginning of the writing; they may differ in their
requirements.

        Candidates should remember that completed theses
will be read not only by the committee and examiners
but also by others using the library or, if they are in
other institutions, through abstracts, microfiches, and
the like. In arts education, prospective readers may
come from a wide variety of disciplines. As a result,
academic jargon should be kept to a minimum. There is
nothing wrong - but a great deal right - with writing
good, clear prose that everyone can understand.

SOME TECHNIQUES

        Thesis writing includes techniques that are not
the same as for writing a book. The following may help:

A   Keep the same focus throughout.
        This is best achieved by ensuring that all
writing is centered on the thesis question. Many theses
in Education (specifically in Curriculum) are arguments
or intellectual debates. Thus they must be logical; one
point should lead to the next.

B   "Tops and tails."
        In each chapter, the Introduction should
state what will occur. The Conclusion should summarize

                              67

what has happened so far and lead to the next chapter.
Nor is there anything wrong in including brief and
pertinent summaries within chapters where the argument
has been complex. Thesis readers should be given every
help in following the argument.

C   Structure.
              Thesis structures vary according to the
methodologies used. Thus:

*   Hard-nosed   empirical   theses   usually   follow
        closely the experimental method's structure.
*   Methods that are more personally based (e.g.,
        phenomenology) often have an emergent structure.
*   Theses that deal with the history/philosophy of
        arts education sometimes follow the structures of
        those disciplines.
*   Many others have the following type of structure:

1   Abstract (written last)
2   Introduction
        -       problematic, limitations and methodology
                stated
        -       general issues to be addressed
3   Review of the Literature
        -       literature of X and Y (at least)
        -       all references that are used in the thesis
                should be contained in the review
4   The Thesis Question
5   Methodology
        -       why this method was chosen
        -       the method described
        -       descriptions of tasks accomplished
        -       for theses with data include: the criteria
                for data, manner of collection, and method
                of analysis
        -       effectiveness of the method
6   Results
7   Discussion of results
8   Conclusion including significance
        Footnotes
        Bibliography

There are many variations on this form. The Style Sheet
required by a particular institution can indicate, in
addition to the details of the style of writing (how to
prepare footnotes, bibliography, and so forth), ways of
structuring the thesis. Candidates in Fine Arts may
possibly have a choice of styles between two (i.e., if
the topic overlaps with another academic discipline).

CONCLUSION

Candidates should keep in mind that, for many years, they will be known by others in arts education for the quality of their thesis. This is the case for large issues like the value of the study for the field, and minutiae like accuracy in the footnotes and the bibliography.

While committee members and examiners are always concerned to keep standards in the field high and will attempt to ensure the quality of the thesis and also prevent small mistakes, the candidate is responsible for them. In the final analysis the responsibility for the thesis and its subsequent reputation remains in the hands of the candidate.

CHAPTER 7

THE EVALUATION OF ARTS PROGRAMS

"Could a greater miracle take
place than for us to look
through each other's eyes for
an instant"
                        - Thoreau

The majority of inquiries in arts education are
program evaluations. While this is not the case with
theses and dissertations, many of these are program
based. However, it is certainly so for those inquiries
funded by the various levels of government and other
agencies. Program evaluations have different emphases
also according to the country of origin of a study.

This chapter will consider program studies while
Chapter 8 will examine other forms of inquiry.

BACKGROUND

BRITAIN

Educational research generally shows a different
bias as between Britain and the United States. While
both inherit the empirical tradition, they do so in a
somewhat different fashion. The British tradition is in
line with Bacon and Mill (and thus inductive) on the
one hand, and with Locke, Berkeley and Hume (and thus
perceptual) on the other - so arts education studies
tend to explicate the particular.

Educational inquiry in the United States, while
empirical, is strongly influenced by John Dewey (whose
dissertation was on Hegel) and the determinism of the
"social behaviourism" of G.H.Mead on the one hand, and
by the "mechanical behaviourism" of Watson and Skinner
on the other. As all are deductive, inquiries into arts
education in the United States tend to emphasize the
general when compared to Britain.

For most of the century, British inquiry in arts
education mainly existed in theses or the rare official
reports at a national or regional level. As curricula
are school-based (influenced by national examinations),

71

research was focused on the particulars of classrooms. Thus both inquiry and program development were looked at through the lens of learning/teaching strategies.

In the mid-1960's, several changes brought about some alterations in arts education inquiry. Nationally the Ministry of Education began internal evaluation projects on programs: these were examined over all jurisdictions and discussed "the state of the arts" in classrooms; they were intended to provide "a snapshot" of the work in the whole country. The few that were made public were highly influential, particularly on classroom practice.

More recently some Schools Council reports have examined the particulars of learning and instruction in the arts, together with the national implications for program design and assessment. Further, the Gulbenkian Foundation has also looked at specific arts issues as they affect education. Two innovations have prepared teachers to ask genuine research questions of practical experience: the opening and development of regional "teachers' centres," and the establishment of graduate diplomas (now degrees) in arts education.

UNITED STATES

Prior to World War II most U.S. arts education investigators were trained in Europe. Changes began about mid-century: in 1949 a group of arts educators published the first "Research Bulletin" and the U.S. Office of Education then appointed an arts education officer. In 1950 Viktor Lowenfeld began the training of "objective" researchers in visual arts education at Pennsylvania State University.

President John Kennedy had a high policy priority for the arts. He made some key appointments: Francis Keppel as Commissioner for Education; and under him, Kathryn Bloom in 1963 became Director of the new Arts and Humanities Program. This supported nearly 200 research and development projects between 1965 and 1970 (Madeja, 1978a). These events were followed by research conferences on music (1964) and on visual arts education (1965); the first was attended by Jerome Bruner, Ralph Tyler, and other social scientists but no one from arts education! The result was a blossoming of research for a few years with two emphases: (1) the use of many standard scientific methods; and also (2) both

72

curriculum development and program evaluation (Hoffa, in: Madeja, 1977: 61-80).

During the political unrest in the late 1960's, the structures for the arts at the federal level were totally reorganized and the funds for arts education research mostly dropped into the cracks between various categories. However the new CEMREL Aesthetic Education Program (with others) was funded. For the next fifteen years, CEMREL continued to promote arts curriculum, program and teacher development - as did foundations (e.g., JDR 3rd Fund, Kettering Foundation, etc.) and state and local governments, some supported by federal funds. One example is the Alliance for Arts Education which funded fifty small projects annually. Although other forms of research were scantily supported from the 1970's, curriculum and program projects continued.

The Reagan administration limited funds for arts education. CEMREL's funds, for example, were withdrawn and there were other funding restrictions, Currently learned journals in music, drama, visual arts, and also aesthetic education are published in the United States.

CANADA & AUSTRALIA

In comparison, program evaluation in Canada and Australia has been miniscule in arts education. Even university research hardly existed for most of this century. Program evaluations did not begin to have any research strength in either country until the 1980's.

In the 1970's in Australia, a cluster of high calibre program projects were undertaken in Melbourne, centered on the Drama Resource Centre, and others began elsewhere including at the federal level. These tended to be more inductive in the British style but recently American models have begun to be used. In recent years, centered around specific universities, thesis research in arts education has developed significantly.

There were a few more theses in Canada, some in French but most in English, and these have recently increased with some rapidity. Graduate programs are, however, small in comparison with those in the United States. Ontario began to fund program evaluations in 1979 and there are now curriculum documents in the arts that are built on solid foundations. Canada publishes only a learned journal in visual arts education.

EVALUATION APPROACHES

Broadly speaking, there are two basic styles of approach to program evaluation: (1) preordinate; and (2) responsive. These represent extreme positions: many assessors combine the types. The key to the differences between the approaches lie in the evaluators' diverse assumptions about education.

QUANTITATIVE (PREORDINATE) EVALUATION

Preordinate evaluators tend to stress numbers and quantitative measures. Ralph Tyler, Benjamin Bloom and James Popham are leaders in this style of evaluation.

Those who inquire into programs quantitatively attempt to make their reports coherent by basing them on specific objectives. These are considered to be the important purposes of education and programs are thus evaluated as to whether they did, or did not, achieve these objectives. This judgment is based on specific student behaviour which, it is assumed, evaluators can assess through preordinate measures.

Common research tools used include quantitative achievement and performance tests, observation check lists, and measures of specific outcomes. Often the conclusion is a final written report. Because of the preordinate evaluator's ties to experimental psychology, the project and the report can be regarded as stimuli to which students or teachers are expected to respond.

Preordinate evaluations are best used when the evaluator needs to know that specific goals have been reached, or that specific ends have been achieved. They are least successful when issues have to be discovered, when changes occur in the purposes of programs, or when individual differences and unique viewpoints must be considered.

Many early evaluations were tackled in this way, particularly in the United States, but this has been less so in recent years. Today, totally preordinate evaluations of arts programs are often likely to be conducted by those specializing in general evaluation who have little sensitivity to or experience in modern arts education.

QUALITATIVE (RESPONSIVE) EVALUATION

Responsive evaluators use a more naturalistic, descriptive or qualitative approach. The leaders in this methodology are Robert E.Stake, Louis M.Smith and Stanley S.Madeja.

They are liable to begin not with the overtly stated objectives of a program but with its activities. From what is happening, they allow the implicit and explicit intentions of the program to emerge.

In its simplest form, this type of evaluation is usually based on human observation and perspectives: the observation and description of activities through many different research modes (see Chapter 5); the preparation of apt, brief descriptions, portrayals, audio-visuals, etc., and the informal responses (of which records are kept) of the teachers, administrators and/or parents to them.

Responsive evaluators are liable to think that what teachers and others say to them reflects their own practical knowledge. The evaluator then prepares either a final report or various partial reports (perhaps in a variety of media) according to the needs of the client. In contrast to the quantitative evaluator, he or she concentrates on natural and complex description (as vs. simplified categories), on existing/revealed metaphors, paradoxes and ambiguities (rather than binary either/or answers), and on the multiplicity of many aesthetic experiences (instead of abstract analysis).

Responsive evaluations are usually best used when the client is concerned with values: the need to search for understanding of particular issues, to find out any student change, to aid in decision-making, to discover if the "climate" is right, to identify any problems of learning and/or teaching, consider human inter-actions, and so on. They are least successful when the client requires cause-and-effect answers, the investigation of pre-determined hypotheses and reliable measures of any individual and/or group achievement.

Increasingly, this style of evaluation is used in arts programs. This is because the style both flexibly relates and adapts to individual differences as well as the unexpected in programs - a specific feature of the arts - and because the programs, like the evaluative mode, are primarily concerned with value and quality.

Although responsive evaluators may, where it is necessary, use preordinate tools for particular program elements, the reverse is not normally the case. Indeed quantitative practitioners are likely to think that any responsive techniques are "subjective" and "soft." In extremis, the two forms of assessment result from the individual's basic assumptions about the purposes of education and inquiry - as between Descartes, Mill, and Skinner on the one hand compared with Heraclitus, Kant and Heidegger on the other.

VARIATIONS

There are many variations on these two types of evaluation. Indeed, the ideal investigator would likely establish a unique methodology for each single project.

Elliot Eisner (1972) has suggested variations in assessments of arts programs:

1   Expressive Objectives.
He urges the consideration of expressive objectives: the outcomes of an activity planned by the teacher or the student in forms of thinking-feeling-acting that are of his or her own making. These are individual for each learner; they are evaluated after the learning experience - that is, through Knowledge ABOUT, when reflection about the experience occurs.

2   Three Images of Outcomes.
Evaluation should, he says, include images of the types of outcomes that are the product of the teaching/learning situation: content- and teacher- and student-specific outcomes.

3   Criticism Models.
Subsequent upon the view of John Mann and Edward Kelly that literary criticism is very similar in purpose, process and impact to evaluation, Eisner has encouraged evaluations in a variety of critical modes - literary, artistic, dramatic, etc. This is close to the view of Heraclitus, Heidegger and many others that the actual and mundane world co-exists with and is revealed by fiction ("the play world,""the aesthetic world").

There are a plurality of attitudes to curriculum and programs. There are (at least) two ways to judge the differences in views of critics and evaluators:

76

1   Inferences can be made between content and
     methodology.
2   Judgments can be made as to the explanatory
     power of the criticism or assessment.

There are a series of concepts drawn from aesthetic
criticism which can be used to investigate the nature
of evaluation: metaphor, point of view ("voice"), plot
("order"), and theme. Willis (1978: 140-465) provides a
series of case studies that illustrate the plurality of
attitudes to evaluation.

All the variations that we have so far discussed
have been related directly to qualitative methods. But
how far have quantitative notions come in adjusting to
qualitative needs?

Even science programs should be based on methods
that are qualitative. Howard Russell (in Kase-Polisini,
1985: 95-110) shows that it is not only arts programs
that need responsive evaluations. He considers a famous
evaluative study - the SIMS project of the IEA about
mathematics in various countries. The methodology used
in this project promises to be potent for the arts. It
used program monitoring rather than individual student
monitoring as it examined:

1   The intended curriculum - what the teacher is
     officially expected to teach and the student is
     expected to learn.
2   The implemented curriculum - what the teacher
     actually "implements" in the classroom.
3   The attained curriculum - what the student
     actually learns.

Across jurisdictions (countries in the case of SIMS,
but conjecturally across provinces/states or school
boards, etc.) there was a commonly agreed "pool" of
items that represented the content of the subject (that
is, mathematics for SIMS). Comparisons were then made
between issues 1, 2, and 3 above with the items in the
"pool." The advantages of such a methodology are that
it uses the sample survey method of gathering data and
that the data collected are not student-specific. This
method of program assessment, says Russell, might well:

          open up the possibilities for new
          types of items and instruments in
          the arts which more truly focus
          attention on the objectives of the

77

arts than has been possible with
traditional test items which fit
neatly into the every-pupil survey
studies which have characterized
evaluations in the past.

EVALUATION STRATEGIES

The evaluation of arts programs is notoriously
elusive. It has to be comprehensive; that is, it must
recognize the many factors that characterize the events
(teaching/learning of arts education) in schools. These
complexities seriously affect evaluation strategies.

DIFFICULTIES

Difficulties cluster around the following issues:

1   Quantitative/qualitative, as above.
2   The transitory nature of the activities.
         Evaluations must occur while the events
     are taking place. In many cases, recording events
     (on film, tape, etc.) changes the nature of the
     arts activities.
3   Multiple learnings.
         Although generally true in all education,
     the arts specifically improve multiple learnings
     at any one time - cognitive, affective, social,
     aesthetic, psycho-motor.
4   Immediate/long-term learnings.
         The arts bring immediate learnings but a
     number of the most significant are long-term.
5   Process/product.
         Values in arts programs must be judged in
     terms of both the personal/group process and the
     external and public nature of the form. Values of
     arts educators differ as to their relative impor-
     tance, although they generally agree that process
     is of greater importance with young children.

In order to grapple with these issues the evaluator
must make some broad decisions as to strategies.

INITIAL QUESTIONS

Evaluators must ask two initial questions that
are complementary to one another:

1   What particular issues must the evaluation deal
        with?
            In order to be effective, an evaluation
        will eventually have to concentrate on one, or a
        few, question(s). If many issues are involved, a
        hierarchy must be evolved or the final report
        will be too complex to be efficient.

2   Who requires the evaluation and for what purpose?
            The evaluation should be of service to a
        specific person or persons. For this to be the
        case, the assessment must address the concerns of
        the client which, as they may be both implicit
        and explicit, may require the evaluator to spend
        some time discovering what they are.

OPERATIONAL PRINCIPLES

        These two prime questions must be developed into
operations that work. In order for the evaluator to
address the questions while grappling with the many
issues of an arts program, he or she needs effective
strategies.

        One effective tool for arts programs is the guide
developed by the Ontario Ministry of Education (1981)
that indicates the following operational principles:

1   Evaluation should recognize the multiple reality
        of an aesthetic experience.
2   Evaluation should be matched to the purpose and
        nature of aesthetic activity.
3   Evaluation should be conducted in conjunction
        with learning and instruction; it should not be
        an activity divorced from them.
4   Evaluation should focus on both the explicit and
        implicit needs of the client.
5   Evaluation should be a continuous, progressive
        and ongoing process which follows the growth and
        learning of students over a significant period of
        time.
6   Evaluation should be varied both in purpose and
        technique to obtain information on the different
        aspects of the learning process and the nature of
        the program.
7   Evaluation should be communicated in clear and
        concise forms to both its primary audience (i.e.,
        the client) and its secondary audience (all those
        involved in the program, i.e., the students and

the teachers, administrators, principals, parents and others).

8   Evaluation should, wherever possible, equip the students to evaluate their own human interests, abilities and achievements.

DISTINCTIONS OF STYLE

Evaluators need to make distinctions between the different styles of judgments, as indicated by Michael Scriven as follows:

1   Worth vs. Function.
        Inquiries may differ as to whether their purpose is to discover the worth of a program (but views will differ considerably as to the nature of "worth" according to various people's tacit assumptions), or to discover processes of functional relationships.
2   Comparative vs. Non-comparative.
        Some evaluations will compare a program with other programs. Some will not.
3   Aims vs. Content.
        A program evaluation may judge the effect of its objectives, methods, content or assessment or all of these. If it judges the adequacy of the aims (or objectives) then the criteria of relatability, uniqueness, and perceptual power may be used. On the other hand, the evaluation may judge the worth of a program's content; the criteria may be the practical limits, the student developmental factors, the social relevance, instrumental value, and/or the intrinsic value (Efland, 1973).

TYPES OF EVALUATION

Michael Scriven was also the first to indicate the types of program evaluation as: (1) diagnostic; (2) formative; and (3) summative.

DIAGNOSTIC

Diagnostic evaluations are required by various educational jurisdictions in order to provide initial information to set program activities in action. These can vary in scale between the need to:

1   establish a policy (province/state-, board- or
        school-wide) that enables a program to come into
        existence - usually through a needs-assessment;
2   assess individual students' needs in relation to
        a program, or programs, usually through:
        a   observation of students in arts activity;
        b   personal interviews;
        c   attitude scales, etc.

FORMATIVE

        Formative evaluations are normally required to
provide information as to:

1   the functioning of an existing program;
2   the possible functioning of a new program of
        which other models are in existence.

These evaluations provide:

a   information for the further planning of courses/
        programs that have already begun as, for example,
        when required by those developing curricula;
b   for teachers and students as to:
        *   the progress being made to fulfil the aims of
             the program;
        *   which skills/attitudes are satisfactory and
             which need improvement.

Methodologies vary. They should be chosen from amongst
the display given in Chapter 5 through which it is well
possible to obtain information of teachers' views about
their students' behaviour, work, strengths and weaknes-
ses. Questions relative to drama education are given in
Ontario government documents (1981: 22-23). Some useful
techniques with students include: direct observation,
interviews, tapes or films, and journals.

SUMMATIVE

        A summative evaluation is primarily intended to
aid users of a program, such as teachers and administrators. It normally occurs at the end of a program (or
unit, course, etc.) It addresses the questions:

1   What has the program achieved?
2   What have the students achieved?

While appropriate methodologies are given in Chapter 5, the most useful techniques include observation reports on students' progress, and personal evaluation reports by students. Other possible (and more quantitative) techniques include teacher devised tests based on the intentions of the arts program, and the holistic marking of (any) presentations or displays. Some questions useful to drama educators are given in Ontario government documents (1981: 23).

EXAMPLES OF PROGRAM EVALUATIONS

Before we briefly examine some examples of arts program evaluations, it is worth reiterating that too much must not be expected of them. This is for the following reasons:

1   Arts activities, and students' learnings in them, are notoriously difficult to evaluate.
2   Quantitative methods are usually too gross and too mechanical to capture the essence of arts programs.
3   Qualitative evaluations, while they are rational perspectives on events (in line with contemporary science and philosophy), do not provide cause-and-effect results or give absolute "truth." But they do provide clients with practical knowledge of the programs.
4   Only in rare cases is an arts evaluation project funded to an adequate extent. Thus in many cases, evaluators must trim the scope of the evaluation to fit the available budget; and that can mean "cutting corners," which is never satisfactory.

It is worth reminding ourselves that most arts program evaluations are essentially practical affairs: their purpose is to be of practical use. In the actual world, not everything is perfect; but as long as we remember that these evaluations are intended for the practical judgments of our clients, we can produce evaluations that are of value.

Most of the major program evaluations that took place in the United States during the 1960's and early 1970's are reviewed by Stake (1975). Their details will not be rehearsed here but the reader is well advised to consult them. They include examples that are still of considerable use.

82

Those discussed below were program evaluations for which I acted as Principal Investigator (PI) or Co-Investigator (CI). In some but not others, one or more Research Officers (RO) were used.

THE HAMILTON PHILHARMONIC INSTITUTE (HPI)

Client: Ontario Arts Council (OAC).
Time: 2 years (1975-76).
Purpose: To examine whether the program met its intentions.
Funds: Middle scale.

The HPI was a one-year full-time training program for young musicians with an existing Music B.F.A., and had just been initiated when the PI visited the site for the first time. The program aimed to provide the students with the type of high-calibre experience that was thought necessary for their future careers as professional musicians:

1 as members of a professional orchestra (Hamilton Philharmonic <HPO>, conductor Boris Brott);
2 as members of small professional ensembles;
3 as entrepeneurs of community music events (in schools, malls, factories, etc.);
4 as learners with visiting musicians distinguished in the above activities.

The program was organized and supervised by two members of The Canadian Brass, with direct links to the HPO.

The HPI received direct funding from the OAC who wished the evaluation to include a recommendation about future funding based on the criterion as to whether the program met its stated aims and objectives.

In initial discussions with the Director OAC and the HPI faculty, it was decided that the evaluation should be: qualitative in approach; formative in type; and a case study in a phenomenological manner.

In practice, the project became a fairly typical responsive evaluation in the manner described by Stake (1975). The PI and the RO visited the participants on site and (for the various styles of performance) in the field: for several hours at a time; on an average of 2 or 3 times a week in terms; and for 2 years. During the visits, they: kept continuous personal records; engaged in dialogue with all the faculty, staff, students, the

83

conductor of the HPO, visiting musicians, audiences, etc.; and observed/documented critical incidents as they occured. Where possible, the PI and RO discussed their current perspective with all concerned using many brief outlines, portrayals, charts and diagrams. The responses were also documented.

As the evaluation continued, the nature of the HPI program changed - often in response to the ongoing discussions with the PI and RO. In many ways, they were informational pipelines between the various groups and individuals. While the odd problem (related to content, instrumental practice time, curriculum implementation, and so forth) occurred and was changed, the main issues that arose were social and organizational:

1   the amount of time devoted to administration by faculty members who, being famous and distinguished performers in their own right, had many other engagements; and
2   particular issues of inter-personal communication between faculty/staff/students.

The first was difficult to resolve but the second, once identified, became a recognized task that had to be addressed by the groups.

Even so, the program was highly successful and it was recommended that funding should be continued.

DESIGN EDUCATION
Client: Design Canada (DC); The Department of Industry,
       Trade & Commerce, the Government of Canada.
Time: 1 year (1977).
Purpose: To examine the most effective strategy for DC
       to intervene in educational programs introducing
       the basic notions of design education, and at
       what level.
Funds: Large scale.

In Canada, the federal government does not have jurisdiction over school programs which remain entirely a provincial matter. It can and does intervene through a variety of ancillary projects; e.g., exhibitions, special events for students, training programs, etc. The Design Council of Canada had serious concerns about the lack of design education in schools, colleges and universities leading to a lack of good Canadian professional designers in many fields. Given the available

84

funds of Design Canada for intervention, the research question was: What strategy would be the most effective and influential?

It was decided that a diagnostic evaluation would be the most appropriate style of investigation with Grounded Theory as the best methodology. Given the wide differences in provincial educational structures and systems, I visited selected sites in Canada (chosen by specific criteria as Vancouver, Winnipeg, Toronto and Halifax) and interviewed many "experts" (e.g., those who understood the concepts underlying design education in various contexts, including educational settings). These included:

*   professional designers (industrial, commercial, etc.);
*   professional design educators;
*   educational administrators and teachers.

For example, the Winnipeg respondents were:

*   5 professional designers;
*   4 faculty members of a university Department of Design;
*   3 provincial educational administrators;
*   2 school board administrators, and
*   11 teachers at different levels of the education-al system.

Interviews were taped and open-ended giving respondents wide latitude to make recommendations. These were typed up immediately as anonymous and colour-coded by theme and content. The initial analysis was made by site and a subsequent analysis was made of the total responses.

The final written report showed:

1   There were insignificant differences in response according to province.
2   The recommended method of intervention was for long-term rather than short-term ends: at the pre-school and primary levels through in-service teacher-education projects ("notions of design education must be understood at the earliest possible age to be genuinely effective").
3   Styles of possible projects were then detailed.

THEATRE DEPARTMENT: UNIVERSITY OF NEW MEXICO (UNM)
Client: as above.
Co-Investigators: Dr.Jack Morrison, Richard Courtney.
Time: 1 week, 1978.
Purpose: To re-vitalise the undergraduate program.
Funds: Small-scale.

The CI's discussed with The Dean and the Department Head the parameters of the review. There had been some concern expressed that re-vitalization was wanted. The clients required that the project should activate faculty members to evaluate the existing program and, if possible, design a new program that had relevance to student needs. It was thus a formative evaluation.

The method chosen was experiential. The two CI's were in attendance at a 3-day "retreat" of faculty and senior undergraduates. The first half-day was planned in detail. From 9.00 to 10.00 a.m. on Day 1, the Head reviewed the background and need, and the CI's told of programs in similar institutions and the needs they had aimed to meet. Immediately thereafter, those attending broke up into discussion groups, each group identifying and listing the particular needs of the program at UNM. The CI's "floated" between groups, responding to any questions, acting as catalysts, and assisting members to come to decisions. After lunch, each group reported back to the whole. The result was a series of various "emergents": issues that had to be addressed for the process to continue. Discussion groups were re-formed to address these emergents – and so the process went on with the CI's making summary statements only when it was considered necessary.

The final "report" was to the Dean and the Head at the end of the experiential process when the group as a whole orally presented "their" new program. This was fully documented and presented to the clients.

DRAMA DEPARTMENT, MELBOURNE STATE COLLEGE, AUSTRALIA
Client: as above.
Time: 2 months full-time, 1979.
Purpose: To assess the Department's program.
Funds: Middle scale.

The College prepared drama teachers (elementary and secondary) in various concurrent programs: 4-year full-time B.Ed.; 2-year part-time graduate Diploma; and M.A.. Additionally there were short courses for those

in non-drama programs. The Department had recently lost
its long-term Head who had established it about 15
years before. It was agreed with the Principal and the
Acting Department Head that I should become Visiting
Fellow with various duties, the largest of which was a
formative evaluation.

It was also agreed that the final report would be
of two parts: (1) internal faculty program assessments
(experiential in the same way as with the UNM project,
above); and that these would be incorporated into (2) a
written analytic evaluation which I would prepare. I
have described elsewhere (Courtney, 1980: 106-08) the
faculty's evaluation process of the secondary program;
similar types of assessment were made of the various
other programs. These were fully documented.

In preparation for the written evaluation, I was
a participant in many classes and conducted many open-
ended interviews with:

*   senior administrators at the federal and state
        levels, the Principal and the Vice-Principals,
        and distinguished arts educators in the state, in
        order to provide the necessary background about
        the relation of policy and funding (past, present
        and future) to the Department's program;
*   the Acting Department Head, Department faculty
        members, and faculty in other Departments having
        direct connections with the Drama Department; and
*   representative samples of students in programs
        and courses.

In each case, I made full notes which became the data
of the study. I subjected this to a Grounded Theory
type of analysis. When the final written report was
presented, the documentation of the faculty's internal
evaluations were attached as appendices.

THE "LEARNING THROUGH THE ARTS" PROJECT
Client: Ministry of Education (MOE), The Government of
        Ontario.
Principal Investigators: Richard Courtney and Paul
        Park.
Time: 1 year, 1980.
Purpose: To discover student learnings through the arts
        in "the general program of studies," primary and
        junior levels (P/J) of the schools of Ontario.
Funds: Large scale.

This formative evaluation of P/J programs was required by the MOE to act as informative documentation for a variety of purposes:

A   to provide a general picture of the arts in the P/J classrooms in Ontario;
B   as background for the preparation of provincial guides, board curricula, and school programs in all subjects in the province;
C   for "general subjects" teachers (responsible for the arts) in lesson preparation and instruction;
D   for arts teachers who required advocacy background to make their case to administrators, parents and the public within a political climate of "back to the basics" and accountability.

For the purposes of the inquiry, the term "the arts" included general arts, music, visual art, drama and dance.

The method chosen was an adaptation of Grounded Theory and included:

1   A review of the literature, plus theme analysis of the indicated learnings through the arts.
2   Identification of a sample of teachers who were responsible for "highly active" arts programs at the P/J level:
     *   by being named by at least two "experts";
     *   by region and locality.
3   Open-ended interviews with these teachers about learning through the arts, and observation of their classes to see whether what they said did in fact match with what happened.
4   Open-ended interviews with arts consultants of the identified teachers on the same theme.
5   Typing of data as anonymous (as at 3 and 4).
6   Analysis of data using grounded theory methodology (colour coding, etc.) according to:
     *   separate grades and divisions;
     *   separate general arts and specific arts;
     *   the data as a whole.
7   Comparison of data analysis with the literature review (as at 1. above).
8   Preparation of final report that:
     *   described learning through the arts in the P/J programs in Ontario;
     *   documented the values of the teachers and administrators responsible;

*   made generalizations about the nature and
        conditions of both learning and programs.
9   Printing and publication of final report: first
        published by MOE in 3 volumes; subsequently Vol.1
        was reissued by the voluntary drama and visual
        arts teacher associations in Ontario for their
        members.

Amongst the various appendices was information useful
to teachers which had been secured by the project but
was not directly related to the study (e.g., a list of
all the arts curriculum documents published by the many
school boards in Ontario). The abstract includes the
following:

> Music and Art are taught in the Pri-
> mary and Junior Divisions of schools
> in the sample but the teaching of Dra-
> ma is less widespread and Dance even
> less so. The majority of school boards
> sampled have a coordinator or consul-
> tant for the arts. Although there is
> support for the arts, high priority is
> not given for teacher development in
> the arts, nor to special arts programs
> for the gifted or those with learning
> handicaps.
>
> The study showed that arts prog-
> rams assist learning in the general
> program of studies by improving per-
> ception, awareness, concentration,
> uniqueness of thought styles, expres-
> sion, inventiveness, problem-solving,
> confidence, self-worth and motivation.
> It also showed that there was a consi-
> derable degree of transfer of learning
> from arts programs to: (a) learning
> and learning readiness in other sub-
> jects; and (b) life and social learn-
> ing. There were, however, differences
> in transfer according to the subject
> base of arts programs. The study also
> showed that there are specific sequen-
> tial learnings through arts programs
> but, as the teachers had little aware-
> ness of the theories of developmental
> stages, the design and implementation
> of school arts programs were not al-
> ways perceived as adequate in relation

to developmental theory. This observation raises issues about the pre-service and in-service arts programs available for teachers. The literature in the field supported the above findings of the survey.

The overwhelming majority of teachers of arts programs regard themselves as generalists and not as specialists. Few have special spaces in which to teach, and the average time available for arts subjects varies between approximately one-and-a-quarter hours and less than half-an-hour per week. Over half of the teachers instruct classes other than their own and the majority have local curriculum guides available and have access to consultants in their area. Although most teachers integrate their arts programs with non-arts subjects, very few have an Integrated Arts program and those that do tend to be kindergarten teachers.

The main body of the report gave details of these and other issues. Although the report was received most enthusiastically by the clients, teachers, administrators and a number of parents, it was criticised by a few quantitative researchers, mainly on the grounds that the teacher sample (over 60) was not large enough. The fact that the Grounded Theory literature indicates that, in using the appropriate criteria, 60 would be too many, did not alter these mechanists' views!

THE "TEACHER EDUCATION IN THE ARTS" PROJECT
Client: The Joint Council on Education, Toronto.
Co-Investigators: Richard Courtney, David Booth, John Emerson and Natalie Kuzmich.
Time: 1 year, 1984.
Purpose: To discover the present needs of pre-/in-service, and graduate programs in arts education for teachers, with specific reference to those at the Faculty of Education, The University of Toronto (FEUT), for pre-/in-service, and those at the Ontario Institute for Studies in Education (OISE), for graduate programs.
Funds: Small scale.

This formative evaluation of teacher education in the arts was considerably under-funded but was welcomed by the CI's, who backed it with additional resources because it directly addressed the programs in which they worked. At the same time, it was acknowledged that the limited funds and resources meant that the project was "a probe" rather than an authoritative and well funded investigation.

To ensure its comparative validity an external Advisory Committee was established. This consisted of: three consultants (one each in Music, Art and Drama) who were distinguished in arts teacher education and were fully aware of the situation across Canada; and three school board representatives (one each in Music, Art and Drama) with considerable experience of arts teacher education in Ontario. This Advisory Committee met at the beginning of the project, monitored the process, and met at the end to discuss the details of the final report.

The survey of the literature revealed the lack of studies in the area. Grounded Theory methodology was used to select teachers (by sample, criteria being the most articulate) in each arts subject currently attending the programs concerned: they were interviewed at least twice, once at the beginning and once at the end, of their particular program. Documentation was made anonymous. After the normal colour coding, analysis, etc., the final report showed amongst other things:

1 The needs of arts teacher education are highly complex with variables including:
    *   the age stage of the school students;
    *   the particular art form practised;
    *   the educational level of the teachers;
    *   the type of program; and
    *   the educational context.
2 The necessary components in the education of arts teachers are:
    *   general education;
    *   education in teaching - theory and practice of both teaching and teaching in the arts; and
    *   education in the arts - both practice and theory.
3 Careful sequencing of learnings in the various stages of arts teacher education is essential, specifically within the current stages in Ontario which are:

91

```
    *       undergraduate degree;
    *       B.Ed. - 1 year pre-service;
    *       Part 1 Certification - Summer in-service;
    *       Part 2 Certification - Summer in-service;
    *       Part 3 Specialist Certification - Summer
            in-service;
    *       M.Ed., or M.A.;
    *       Ed.D., or Ph.D.
```
The institutions concerned (FEUT and OISE) should cooperate to this end.

4   Programs should be carefully designed to meet the needs of the clients' teaching contexts, thus:
    *   for General programs/Specific programs (e.g., gifted, talented, special, etc.);
    *   for specialists/generalists/aides, etc.

5   Arts experiences in such programs should include those with new media, forms and technologies, and should balance:
    *   spontaneity/skill;
    *   creativity/appreciation.

6   All programs should include the study of child development focused on the division level taught by the teacher. This should include not only cognitive development (which is commonly taught) but also the perceptual/emotional/feeling modes (which are not commonly taught).

7   All types of existing programs require increased time; and numbers in course sections should be kept to a minimum.

8   All programs should include content on criteria for assessment in the arts.

The study claimed to provide "a glimpse of arts teacher education" with indications for further study. With insufficient research funds for publication, two voluntary associations for arts teachers gave support towards publication and distribution by Bison Books, Sharon, Ontario.

CHAPTER 8

RESEARCH PROJECTS

"A study belongs to the human area
only if its objects becomes accessi-
ble to us through the attitude which
is founded on the relation between
life, expression, and understanding"
- Dilthey

We have seen that the evaluation of arts programs
represents one large group of research projects. While
most assessments are made for clients, it is possible
to evaluate programs through theses although these are
not written for clients - except if an examination
committee might be regarded as "clients"!

This chapter is concerned with research projects
that are not evaluations of arts education programs.
Clearly there are so many types of such projects, and
so many variations of method, that it is impossible to
be comprehensive. By turning again to Chapter 5, we can
see the many possibilities of method. We will address
in this chapter the kinds of research projects that are
most common.

If we return to first principles we see that there
are a series of issues, not already dealt with, which
the beginning arts researcher must consider. Research,
as we have said, is to seek knowledge when:

1   we recognize that the quest is to pursue one view
     on events; and
2   we use rational or empirical methods to address a
     genuine research question.

These principles should be applied to the issues that
follow.

MEASUREMENT RESEARCH

We have already seen that empirical approaches use
quantification and measurement as methods. Although
they are no longer regarded as the only "proper" ways
to research, there remain certain research issues that

may require an empirical approach. If we ask questions like, "How many . . . ?" or, "Does P cause Q to . . . " then measurement will usually be involved.

This applies as much to arts education as to any other aspect of education. It is particularly the case with learning through the arts when issues of applied psychology are addressed. Take the following questions, for example:

* Do creative dramatic activities help to reduce stammering amongst Primary students?
* Does a visual arts program in Grade 1 improve reading ability?
* Do music activities help to improve the learning of a second language?

On the one hand, these questions might be addressed as they were in the "Learning Through the Arts" project (see pp. 87-90): Grounded Theory methods might be used so that "experts" can be asked such questions. But the results (impartial, rational and objective though they may be) may not satisfy everyone's view of "objective truth." On the other hand, an experimental method might be set up with two parallel classes, one receiving the arts treatment and one not and, with a series of tests, the students could be rated, scored, and statistical analyses made. While this method may satisfy those who require mechanical truths, it might also miss many of the subtleties of teaching and learning through the arts. Neither is perfect. Both provide a perspective on events. Which we choose depends on the circumstances in which the research is to be conducted.

Although measurement studies have been developed in each of the arts, the normal initial procedure is as follows:

1   Refine the question so that it is researchable.
2   State the hypothesis/hypotheses:
    * reasons for considering it worthy
    * ways in which it is testable
3   Search for possible measures to be used.
    Instruments or tools for measurement can come from a particular arts field (e.g., music) or from various related fields (e.g., applied psychology) as required.

94

4   Description of the subjects needed for the study.
     Consideration must be given to the chance
     of obtaining the number/type of subjects
     required.
5   Draw up tentative design/plan of action.
     Details of possible research designs are
     given in Borg and Gall (1963, rev.1974:
     Chapters 12-16).
6   Initial description of the way(s) the data will be
     analysed.
     This may reveal issues about: the number
     of subjects, the measures and scoring to
     be used, methods of recording data, etc.
7   Consider:
*   definitions
*   limitations.

Thereafter, the researcher should follow the procedures
recommended by Borg and Gall (1974).

Most intriguingly, there have been some inquiries
in arts education recently that have used measurement
studies but where the researcher was well aware of the
need to capture a holistic experience within a linear
research method.

THE DEVELOPMENTAL DRAMA SCALE (DDS)

An excellent example of the use of quantitative
and measurement methods to capture the quality of arts
experience is the study of Joyce A.Wilkinson (1983) who
evaluated students' involvement (rather than ability or
talent) in creative drama activities in relation to
self-monitoring and hemisphericity. To this end, she
developed the Developmental Drama Scale (DDS).

This is a reliable and valid measure that teachers
can administer easily and quickly within their normal
classroom practices. Subsequently, the DDS was used to
explore what, if any, relationship exists between the
students' involvement in developmental drama and their
hemisphericity.

The approach used was causal-comparative. Three
similar tasks were used as stimuli for simultaneous
group participation, and the tasks were presented by
the respective classroom teachers in five different

95

secondary schools. Appropriate pre- and post-tests were administered. Although there is no claim that the DDS in any way measures all parts of dramatic functioning, it yields six category scores: sensory awareness, concentration, emotional expressiveness, imagination, movement, and communication. To put this another way, these observable behaviours are quantified and analysed systematically. Wilkinson makes the important point that:

> This perspective is fair to all participants since all can progress in degrees of involvement whereas talent and/or ability may be functions of birth and/or environment over which individuals have little control. Involvement is not based on value judgment or indiscriminate favouritism . . . The DDS does, therefore, closely parallel a fundamental precept of the developmental drama process, i.e., drama is for everyone, not just a talented few.

The DDS also indicated that:

1 participants in spontaneous dramatic action are more highly self-monitoring than a non-drama group; thus, they are better prepared for the "theatre of life"; and
2 participants in spontaneous dramatic action are more likely than a non-drama group to process information in a right hemispheric mode.

SURVEY RESEARCH

Researchers have used surveys in their quest for knowledge over many centuries. The ancient Egyptians took population counts and surveys of crop production. Today, similar techniques are used by pollsters, market researchers, economists, political analysts, and so on.

Surveys are often used in educational inquiry as a prime method or as a secondary method to support one aspect of the study. Contrary to some popular opinion, surveys involve more than sending out questionnaires and analyzing them. It is true that the questionnaire and the individual interview are the most common survey

instruments. The major difficulty lies in the obtaining
of standarized information: people do not always tell
all that they know, or tell what easily fits into a
surveyor's categories.

ARTS & EDUCATION IN CANADA

A good example of an arts education survey is that
of Booth and Reynolds (1983) which displayed the arts
curricula throughout Canada by Province. Its purposes
were: to estimate the present level of commonality, and
predict future levels of commonality, in arts education
in Canada; and to facilitate a higher level of inter-
provincial cooperation. Apart from giving arts course
information by province, the study was able to indicate
commonalities in music, visual arts, drama and dance
education, provide a profile of teachers in each of
these arts, indicate teacher education programs and
provincial certification requirements, show provisions
for inservice courses, visiting artists in schools, and
so forth.

POLICY RESEARCH

There are very few research studies that discuss
the relationship between policy and arts education.
There are many studies on cultural policy per se; while
some refer to arts education, few do so in any detail.
One of the leaders in such studies is Ralph A.Smith (in
Madeja, 1977: 305-16).

More common today are "political" studies that
intend to change the cultural policy of a government
(local, regional, national) through advocacy. Usually
these use specific research studies to support their
arguments; there are examples of this style of inquiry
from the United States, Britain, Australia and Canada.

Governments also establish their own inquiries
into policy though, again, there are few contemporary
studies that deal expressly with arts education and
also have a solid research base. An exception is as
follows:

THE "ARTS IN SOCIETY" PROJECT
Client: Alberta Culture.
Time: 3 months, 1973.
Purpose: To assess the current needs in Alberta for the
    arts and arts education as expressed by the
    community.
Funds: Small scale.

The Provincial Department responsible for culture
- Alberta Culture - had arranged for as many provincial
artists and arts educators as possible (many hundreds)
to be in the town of Red Deer for one week in order to:

1   present their work - displays, shows, classes,
     performances, etc.;
2   attend meetings - many each day, with different
     topics - to express their views about cultural
     policy and funding.

The intentions of the research project were:

A   to document all meetings as they occurred;
B   subsequently to analyze the data and present the
     views of those involved.

The documentation was particularly difficult as there
were several meetings taking place at any one time and,
with the limitation of funds, not all reporters were
equally well trained. Nor was the analysis easy: there
were many conflicting views; there was a mixture of
well- and ill-informed views; and, because many of the
speakers went off the given topic, there had to be a
complex system of colour coding prior to the analysis.

The final report was lengthy; it summarized the
issues and made specific recommendations. The Alberta
government used it as background to form subsequent
policy. It also printed and distributed copies to every
library in Alberta.

FIELD RESEARCH

Field studies assume that the site for collecting
the data is within the context of the subjects being
studied. In anthropology, for example, the researcher
is likely to spend long periods "in the field," usually
living with the group to be studied.

Often educational inquiries are so conducted. Many are on a site for some considerable time (often those that are part of counselling, anthropology, sociology), but some are only in the field for brief periods - as when an empirical instrument is applied in a classroom. An example of field research with close connections to the arts is that of Peter McLaren - a case study of one particular school analysed in terms of ritual.

Long-term field research in arts education per se, however, hardly exists. I have explored this method of inquiry for some years to examine both drama and arts education within the ritual of various tribal peoples: long periods with Amerindians of the Pacific Northwest coast of Canada (1968-71) and of the American Southwest (1980, 1984), and shorter periods amongst Australian aboriginals and South Sea islanders. The approach and method has not yet been fully codified and I regard the work so far as a research "probe."

The research method has been both qualitative and observational, with additional information supplied by informants. In an attempt to reduce my own cultural lenses, I have tried to document the observations by using two notions that are common to tribal peoples:

1   art as a distinct category does not exist but is
     an integral part of religious existence - the
     performance of the ritual-myth;
2   what we would call "arts education" is, amongst
     tribal peoples, linked to our other notion of
     "training" - inclusive of "mothering,""play" and
     "initiation" (generalized and specific).

My notes about their arts education, therefore, are in two very loose sets of groupings:

A   religious performance (as arts education);
B   training (as arts education).

Because I am sure that this documentation is not fully satisfactory, some data are coded in more than one group and there is considerable cross-referencing. At the same time, the attempt to exchange one set of cultural lenses for another has, in many instances, been very revealing.

99

This research is ongoing; considerable data has been collected and further field study is designed. So far, at least, it has resulted in a series of papers (Courtney, 1983, 1984, 1985b, 1986a).

SCHOLARLY RESEARCH

Scholarly research relies less on data obtained from direct observation and more on existing evidence. It is also liable to hinge on the scholarly methods of another discipline: history, say, or philosophy.

HISTORICAL

Historical research has been defined in a number of ways, one of the most succint being: "the systematic and objective location, evaluation, and synthesis of evidence in order to establish facts and draw conclusions concerning past events" (Borg and Gall, 1974: 260). As it relies on evidence, historical research uses reason as its approach - "criteria in context" - and is, therefore, objective. The basic steps are:

1   defining the problem and refining the research question;
2   gathering the evidence;
3   evaluating and synthesizing the evidence;
4   providing a rational and accurate account of the problem investigated.

In many cases, this style requires the establishment of a hypothesis; then the research question becomes, "Is it the case that . . . ?"

There have been a number of historical research studies about arts education. There have been far more, however, which cannot be called "research" in the normal sense of this term. To be regarded as genuine educational research, historical inquiry should be:

A   rational and objective;
B   accurate;
C   based on primary sources (documents where the observer was present at the event) shown to be authentic by an examination of the document rather than its content;

D   supported by secondary evidence (documents where
     the observer was not present at the event).

Too many historical studies in arts education in the
past have relied on secondary evidence. Others have not
distinguished between the facts that are shown to be
the case and meaningful generalizations.

     An illustration of the problems in arts education
historical research is a project on which I have been
engaged for some years: an international history of
drama education since 1900. By 1984 I thought (falsely)
that I had gathered sufficient data based on primary
sources to produce a good comparative study. In order
to be sure, however, I wrote to colleagues throughout
the world telling them of the project and asking for
any primary data which I might not have. Within three
months, through the generosity of my colleagues and
their contacts, I was overwhelmed with more primary
sources - boxfuls of which were piled high in my study!
At the time of writing, I still have not completed the
collation of this new evidence. It will be many months
before I can get to the stage of evaluation/synthesis.

     A further illustration of historical approaches is
as a support for other studies. For example, the field
research concerning ritual and arts education (see pp.
99-100) revealed that it required comparisons with many
historical cases. These became so diverse that whole
sub-projects were developed about the ritual of the
ancient Near East, Europe, India, Asia, etc.

PHILOSOPHICAL

     Philosophical research in arts education in many
cases obeys similar parameters to that of history. For
example, a study of the significance of Croce to arts
education might begin from the systematic and objective
location, evaluation, and synthesis of evidence - of
Croce's notions and evidence of his importance to arts
education. The same would apply, but with much more
complexity, to the contemporary notions of process-
form, or spontaneity-skill, in both aesthetics and arts
education.

     Studies in aesthetics and aesthetic education are
rarely funded as research projects. More commonly they
are prepared as scholarly papers for learned journals.

Young scholars should be warned, however, that many of these journals prefer articles on aesthetics per se rather than on arts and aesthetic education.

THEORETIC

Even more difficult is the development of theory in arts education. Where qualitative research methods breed resistance amongst quantitative scientists, the opposition is even greater to pure theory.

But if done well, theoretic research has great value: it can provide insights into many educational problems that cannot be gained by any other method. The most authoritative procedure for theoretic research is as follows:

1   defining the problem and refining the research question;
2   rationally explaining the real need for theoretic research, with evidence of both the need for it and the inability of other methods to answer the question;
3   statement of the theory (hypothesis);
4   provision of an appropriate research framework for the investigation - educational, psychological, anthropological, critical, etc.;
5   location of evidence that supports and contradicts the theory;
6   evaluation and synthesis of the evidence according to the frame-work chosen.

An example is as follows.

THE "AESTHETIC LEARNING" PROJECT
Supported by: Social Sciences & Humanities Research
     Council of Canada.
Time: 1 year, 1984.
Purpose: To develop a theory of aesthetic learning as a
     basis for arts education and for school programs
     generally.
Funds: Middle scale.

1   This project asked, "What is aesthetic learning?"
2   The literature in arts education generally assumes that there is a mode of learning called aesthetic

102

but with insufficient clarity to help the teacher in the classroom. General theories of learning are of little assistance because they are liable to articulate the domains of learning as cognitive/affective/psychomotor without particularizing the aesthetic.

3   The hypothesis was: there is an identifiable aesthetic mode of learning but that it overlaps with other modes.

4   The research methodology chosen was semiotics: the distinction between signifer and signified; and that of General Semiotics (the philosophic issues identified by the distinction) rather than of Specific Semiotics (the issues of particular "languages").

5   The evidence was located in many disciplines: education, the arts, arts education, psychology, anthropology, cultural history, philosophy, and aesthetics, etc.

6   The evaluation and synthesis of the evidence gave support for the hypothesis, showing:

*   there is an identifiable aesthetic mode of learning that is based upon feeling;

*   it operates by judgment and choice;

*   it tacitly infuses the cognitive and, while it is distinct from emotion in many instances, in other cases it links with emotion;

*   there is a specific domain of "aesthetic knowing" which underlies all other forms of knowledge;

*   the structures of aesthetic knowing are based on similarity and are specifically not binary; the initial human structures are whole/part and poles on a continuum;

*   aesthetic knowing is externalized in action which brings about those changes which can be said to be "aesthetic learning";

*   in living experience aesthetic knowing/acting/learning are one whole.

The study goes on to examine a whole series of related issues: metaphor, symbol, dramatic action, sequencing of aesthetic learning, arts education, etc. This theory must be regarded as unproven. To obtain substantiation it must be confirmed by other studies (rational and empirical). These subsequent studies can be designed as longitudinal and commence with infants at birth.

CONCLUSION

"The world of play is necessarily
one of uncertainty and discovery at
every moment, whereas the ambition
of the bureaucrat and the systems-
builder is to deal only with fore-
gone conclusions"
                    - Marshall McLuhan

Being part of contemporary research in arts and
education is an exciting business. Inquiry is now so
flexible and methods are so many that it has been said
that there are as many methods as there are questions.
In the sense used by Heraclitus and Heidegger, this is
to be part of "a play world" - a universe where there
is both mundane actuality and fictional representations
of that actuality.

This excitement may be because arts education came
late to the problem of research. Earlier this century
the battles between measurement and reason were fought
out but the blood of others was spilled. The war was
virtually over when we came to the field. Yet it is not
quite over even today. There are still those who think
that only measurement research is "proper" and we must
be on guard that they do not force us to march to their
drum.

The best way to protect what has already been won
on our behalf is to ensure that our inquiries are both
significant and rigorous. Research must be meaningful:
it must address the large and important issues that
have significance to us as human beings. But it must
also be so executed that those to whom it is directed
(our clients, examiners, colleagues, all the research
community) can respect it. Without that respect the
inquiry is not worth a great deal.

One sign of respect is to treat the inquiries of
others as we would expect them to treat ours. That is
to say, we should ask first: Is this study significant?
and, Is it rigorous? Because it uses a method different
from our own is no reason to denigrate it. We can ask
whether this particular method is the appropriate one
to address this specific question. And then: Was this
method pursued with rigor? That is treating research
with proper respect.

Nor should we condemn a research project because it does not answer a question it did not address. To have validity, an inquiry should address the initial research question; it may, on the way, address various subsidiary questions. But to suggest that it should discuss pears when it has set out to examine apples is far from productive.

In inquiries like program evaluation, we must take into account the needs of the client, the purpose and end in view, the context, and the total support of the project. If funds are severely restricted for such a project, it stands to reason that a program evaluation cannot be exhaustive. Indeed, provided the researcher does not claim that it is so, but has been as rigorous as circumstances permit, then the study is valid.

Some of our gravest problems lie with our brave colleagues who march forward with the word ART blazoned on their banners. "What's the use of research?" they ask. "It is not an art. And arts education is about creating art - nothing else!" Often, there is no one more dangerous than one's friends!

As Picasso said, "Art IS." No one would disagree that what we are all about is the improvement of the students' experiences and learnings in arts education. But inquiries ABOUT arts education are different kinds of beasts from inquiries IN arts education. Like the disguised weasel told the Judge in "Toad of Toad Hall": "I'm a different sort of rabbit!" The artist and the teacher and the researcher aim, in the end, to improve arts education - each in their own way.

APPENDIX

RESEARCH IN CREATIVE ARTS THERAPIES

The creative arts therapies are increasingly used in a wide variety of contexts. Research in this field bears some likeness to inquiries in arts education but, additionally, there are some differences. I have given elsewhere an overview of this in terms of drama therapy (Courtney and Schattner), but it is necessary here to provide some details of the overall conditions for both research and inquiry.

THE USE OF CREATIVE ARTS THERAPIES

The creative arts therapies include the use of creative arts for the purposes of psychological and social health. In practice, they are experientially based: the clients are entirely concerned with their expression in the arts. In this sense, they work with Knowledge IN. Any Knowledge ABOUT is through discussion of their own spontaneous artistic creations.

As one whole field, the creative arts therapies include the sub-fields of music therapy, visual arts therapy, drama/theatre therapy, and dance therapy. In addition there are minor sub-fields where therapies are associated with photography, film and other media.

The creative arts therapies include the use of creative arts in either medical, educational or social contexts:

THE MEDICAL CONTEXT

For patients with mental or physical dysfunctions the creative arts are used in:

1   Diagnosis.
2   Treatment.

In either instance, the work is usually supervised by a medical practitioner although it may be carried out in practice by a creative arts therapist in an adjunct capacity. The work usually takes place in a one-on-one situation or, perhaps, with a small group.

THE EDUCATIONAL CONTEXT

For those attending educational institutions the creative arts are used by teachers in:

1   The General Program of Studies.

The creative arts are most useful for the psychological health of all students. The intrinsic learnings that are fostered by such activities (perception, awareness, concentration, uniqueness of thought style, expression, inventiveness, problem-solving, confidence, self-worth and motivation) are valuable for all persons and are positive forces for human development of all students (Courtney and Park, 1980).

2   Programs of Special Education.

Education programs for special populations each have unique needs for creative arts therapies. The gifted and the mentally and physically handicapped all require particular programs within which the creative arts act in a therapeutic manner. They provide: (a) therapeutic activities for the particular special need; and (b) the positive improvement of psychological and social health (as at 1. above).

THE SOCIAL CONTEXT

The creative arts therapies are valuable in many social contexts: with the aged, with the socially and economically disadvantaged, in multi-cultural contexts, with ex-prisoners and ex-patients, and with self-help groups of all kinds. Arts activities, as we have seen above, lead to both positive social and psychological health and are so used by social leaders of all kinds.

TYPES OF INQUIRY

It is important to distinguish the possible types of inquiry available and suitable for the creative arts therapies. They include:

1   BY KIND OF INQUIRY

The creative arts therapies lend themselves to two kinds of inquiry:

a   assessment of individuals; and
b   evaluation of programs.

Many medical inquiries are through assessment of unique individuals or, at most, small groups of people. Rather in contrast, an inquiry in a particular educational or social context may well evaluate the program per se; if individuals in that context are assessed, it is often to discover the effectiveness of the program.

2   BY DISCIPLINE

The creative arts therapies impinge on a variety of separate disciplines: medicine, the arts, applied psychology, psychotherapy, sociology, anthropology, education and social work amongst others. It is very important for the researcher to select the appropriate research tool for the job in hand. With the different available methods and strategies from the variety of disciplines, this may lead to confusion.

The most appropriate procedure is to:

a   refine the research question accurately;
b   decide whether this is best addressed by a
        quantitative or qualitative methodology
        (see Chapter 5 and pp. 74-78);
c   search the various disciplines for the
        research tool that best meets conditions
        a. and b. above.

It is fair to say that, because the arts therapies have in the past not devised their own appropriate research methodologies, inquiries have been concentrated within quantitative psychological/psychotherapeutic/medical research. Thus many have been causal, mechanical and categoric. In some cases this was quite satisfactory; in some cases, not. Many, indeed, have attempted to achieve a result that the research tool was not capable of achieving.

Supervisors specifically have been limited when indicating research methods suitable for theses. Much may have been due to the limits on methods set by a university Department or a Graduate School. Supervisors would be well advised to seek out and cooperate with graduate faculty in many Departments to widen possible methodologies. I have found that research scholars - at least, good ones - welcome such academic cooperation.

109

Perhaps the greatest lack in the research in this field is that which addresses the arts therapies as arts therapies. That is to say, virtually all studies address a question from outside the field.

Two examples will serve:

a   "Does visual art therapy improve the reading of Grade 4 students?"

This is a mechanistic cause-and-effect question most suitable for the experimental method. It primarily addresses reading. The "treatment" will be activity in visual arts therapy while the testing and the results will be entirely through reading (testing tools from applied psychology and/or education). In terms of the research method, the "treatment" is secondary. It could as well be singing, speaking, listening, learning by phonics, or hitting one's head with a hammer, as much as visual arts therapy.

b   "Does music therapy decrease the auditory hallucinations of paranoid schizophrenics?"

Many of the same issues as at a. are also raised by this question. The primary focus is on an inquiry based on medicine and/or psychology and not on music therapy as such.

This is specifically NOT to say that these are bad questions. On the contrary, they are the basis for perfectly good research questions. But we should also acknowledge them for what they are: they are precisely not questions that are focused upon the creative arts therapies. Both could equally well be asked by applied psychologists.

What does a question that focuses upon the arts therapies look like? That is difficult to answer if only because few such questions have yet to be asked. The field is new and, until this time, it has tended to piggy-back upon other disciplines.

The following are drawn from existing studies and give some indication of questions that focus on the creative arts therapies:

i   What are the necessary conditions in preparing
    creative arts therapists to deal adequately with:
    *   hearing impaired children in schools?
    *   manic-depressive adults as out-patients?
    *   inner-city teenagers in social contexts?

ii What is the relation of spontaneity and skill in
    music (or another art) therapy when improvement
    in the arts is shown by:
    *   a specific client/group/population?

iii Which (of two) creative arts therapies (or which
    of two techniques in one medium) are more condu-
    cive to self-revelation by:
    *   a specific client/group/population?

iv In what ways does a specific technique in music
    (or another art) therapy help:
    *   a specific client/group/population?

v   What are the emergents of a formative evaluation
    of a creative arts program for a specific special
    education class?

vi Which common factors in music and drama therapy
    (or any two) improve feelings of self-worth of:
    *   a specific client/group/population?

It is necessary to note that these questions will need
more precision when they are refined for a specific
situation.

SUMMARY

    In sum, research in the creative arts therapies
should:

1   distinguish between assessment and evaluation;
2   primarily address a problem from the viewpoint of
    the discipline of the creative arts as therapy;
3   develop methodologies where the focus of the
    research is the creative arts activity used in
    therapeutic contexts and not in the service of
    another discipline.

BIBLIOGRAPHY

Allen, Rhianon, and Arthur S.Reber. "Very long term memory for tacit knowledge," Cognition, 8, 2 (June 1980): 175-85.

Anastasi, A., and J.P.Foley, Jr. "An analysis of spontaneous artistic productions by the abnormal," Journal of General Psychology, 28 (1943): 297-313.

Andrade, E.N. Isaac Newton. London: Parrisch, 1952.

Aristotle. The basic works, ed. Richard McKeon. New York: Random House, 1941.

Bacon, Francis. Philosophical works, ed. J.M.Robertson. London: Routledge (1905), 1953.

Barthes, Roland. "The structuralist activity," trans. R.Howard, in: Partisan Review, 34, 1 (Winter 1967): 82-88.

Berger, Peter L., and Thomas Luckmann. The social construction of reality. New York: Doubleday, 1966.

Bergson, Henri. Creative evolution, trans. A.Mitchell. New York: Random House, 1944.

Berkeley, George. A new theory of vision, ed. A.D. Lindsay. London: Dent, 1910.

Bertalanffy, Ludwig von. An introduction to theoretical biology. New York: Harper, 1962.

Best, David. Expression in movement and the arts. London: Lepus, 1974.

Bloom, Benjamin S., J.Thomas Hastings, and George F. Madaus. Handbook on formative and summative evaluation. New York: McGraw-Hill, 1970.

Borg, W., and M.D.Gall. Educational research: An introduction. New York: David McKay, 1963, rev. 1974.

Booth, David, and Howard Reynolds. Arts: A survey of provincial curricula at the elementary and secondary levels. Toronto: Council of Provincial Ministers of Education, 1983.

113

Buber, Martin. I and thou, trans. R.G.Smith. New York: Scribner's, 1958.

Buber, Martin. Martin Buber on theatre, trans. and ed. M.Friedman. New York: Funk and Wagnall, 1969.

Burke, Kenneth. A grammar of motives, and A rhetoric of motives. Cleveland: World Pub. Co., 1961.

Burke, Kenneth. Language as symbolic action. Berkeley, Calif.: University of California Press, 1965.

Campbell, Warren, and Jack Heller. "An orientation for considering models of musical behaviour," in: Hedges, D. (ed.) Handbook of Music Psychology. Lawrence, Kansas: National Association for Music Therapy, 1980.

Camus, Albert. The myth of Sisyphus, trans. J.O'Brien. New York: Knopf, 1955.

Cassirer, Ernst. The philosophy of symbolic forms, trans. R. Mannheim, 3 vols. New Haven: Yale University Press, 1953.

Connelly, F.Michael, and students. Research methods. Monograph. Toronto: OISE, 1980.

Cottle, T.J. Private lives and public accounts. Amherst: University of Massachusetts Press, 1977.

Council for Research in Music Education. Bulletin No.83 (Summer 1985). Urbana, Ill.: School of Music, University of Illinois.

Courtney, Richard. "Drama and aesthetics," British Journal of Aesthetics, 8, 4 (1968): 378-86.

Courtney, Richard. "On Langer's dramatic illusion," Journal of Aesthetics & Art Criticism, 29, 1 (Fall 1970): 11-20.

Courtney, Richard. "A dramatic theory of imagination," New Literary History, 2, 3 (Spring 1971): 445-60.

Courtney, Richard. "Imagination and the dramatic act: Some comments on Sartre, Ryle and Furlong," Journal of Aesthetics & Art Criticism, 30, 2 (Winter 1971): 163:70.

Courtney, Richard. "Theatre and spontaneity," Journal of Aesthetics & Art Criticism, 32, 1 (Fall 1973): 79-88.

Courtney, Richard (ed.) The arts in society. Research report. Edmonton: Alberta Culture, 1973.

Courtney, Richard. Play, drama and thought. London: Cassell; New York: Drama Books, 3rd rev.ed., 1974.

Courtney, Richard. "Imagination and substitution: The personal origins of art," Connecticut Review, 9, 2 (May 1976): 67-73.

Courtney, Richard. "The discipline of drama," Queen's Quarterly, 84, 2 (Summer 1977a): 231-43.

Courtney, Richard. "Goals in drama teaching," Drama Contact, 1, 1 (May 1977b): 5-8.

Courtney, Richard. "Making up one's mind: Aesthetic questions about children and theatre," in: McCaslin, Nellie (ed.) Theatre for Young Audiences. New York: Longman, 1978.

Courtney, Richard. Teaching and the arts: Arts education in Australia, with specific reference to drama education in Victoria. Melbourne: Melbourne State College, 1979a.

Courtney, Richard. "Arts education in Canada," Curriculum, Newsletter of the Canadian Association for Curriculum (November 1979b): 2-5.

Courtney, Richard. The dramatic curriculum. London, Ont.: Althouse Press, University of Western Ontario; London, U.K.: Heinemann; New York: Drama Books, 1980a.

Courtney, Richard. "The crux of the curriculum: The arts as anthropocentrism," in: Condous, Jack, Janferie Howlett and John Skull (eds.) Arts in cultural diversity. Sydney, N.S.W.: Holt, Rinehart and Winston, 1980b.

Courtney, Richard. "Aristotle's legacy: Emotion as related to theatre and children," Indiana Theatre Bulletin, 2, 3 (Winter 1981): 1-10.

Courtney, Richard. Re-play: Studies of human drama in education. Toronto: OISE Press, 1982a.

Courtney, Richard. "Microcosmos: Planning and implementation of drama programs," in: Engel, Martin, and Jerome Hausman (eds.) Curriculum and instruction in arts and aesthetic Education. Fourth Yearbook on Research in Arts and Aesthetic Education. St.Louis: CEMREL, 1982b: 82-110.

Courtney, Richard. "Human performance: Meaning and knowledge," Journal, National Association for Drama in Education (Australia), 8, 1 (1983a): 5-12.

Courtney, Richard. Secret spirits: Ritual performance of Amerindians on Vancouver Island. Paper delivered at the Origins of Theatre Conference, Theatre of Nations, Sofia, Bulgaria, June 1983. Paris: International Theatre Institute (UNESCO), 1983b.

Courtney, Richard. Shamanism on the Pacific Northwest coast of Canada. Paper delivered at the Theatre et Shamanisme Conference, Paris, June 1984. Paris: Centre des Cultures du Monde, 1984.

Courtney, Richard. Aesthetic learning. Research report. Ottawa: Social Sciences and Humanities Research Council of Canada, 1985a.

Courtney, Richard. Rehearsing for life: Teaching drama teachers. Paper delivered at the annual conference, Children's Theatre Association of America, 1985. Toronto, 1985b.

Courtney, Richard. "The dramatic metaphor and learning," in: Kase-Polisini, Judith (ed.) Creative drama in a developmental context. Lanham, MD: University Press of America, 1985c.

Courtney, Richard. "The reality of fiction," Proceedings, Second Annual Conference, 1985, Canadian Society of Aesthetics. Toronto: University of Toronto, 1985d.

Courtney, Richard. "Indigenous theatre: Indian and Eskimo ritual drama." In: Wagner, Anton (ed.) Contemporary Canadian theatre: New world visions. Toronto: Simon and Pierre, 1986a.

116

Courtney, Richard. "Islands of remorse: Amerindian education in the contemporary world," Curriculum Inquiry, 16, 1 (Spring 1986b): 43-64.

Courtney, Richard. Play - The dramatic idea. Forthcoming, 1986c.

Courtney, Richard. "Emergents," Proceedings, Third Annual Conference, Canadian Society of Aesthetics, Winnipeg, 1986. Toronto: University of Toronto, 1986d.

Courtney, Richard, and Paul Park. Learning in the arts. 3 vols. Toronto: Ministry of Education, Government of Ontario, 1981.

Courtney, Richard, and Gertrud Schattner (eds.) Drama in therapy, 2 vols. New York: Drama Books, 1981.

Courtney, Richard, David Booth, John Emerson and Natalie Kuzmich. Teacher education in the arts. Sharon, Ont.: Bison Books, 1985.

Courtney, Richard, David Booth, John Emerson and Natalie Kuzmich (eds.) Basic books in arts education. Sharon, Ont.: Bison Books, 1986.

Croce, Benedetto. Aesthetic, trans. D.Ainslie. London: Peter Owen, repr. 1967.

Darwin, Charles. On the origin of the species by means of natural selection. London: J.Murray, 1859.

Derrida, Jacques. Dissemination, trans. B.Johnson. Chicago: University of Chicago Press, 1981.

Descartes, Rene. The philosophical works of Descartes, trans. E.S.Haldane and G.R.T.Ross, 2 vols. Cambridge: Cambridge University Press, 1931.

Dewey, John. Art as experience. New York: Minton, Balch, 1935.

Dewey, John. Experience and education. New York: Macmillan, 1938.

Diderot, Denis. The paradox of acting. New York: 1957

Efland, Arthur D. "Normative evaluation in aesthetic education." Paper presented to the National Art

Association Conference, San Diego, April 15-20, 1973.

Einstein, Albert. The world as I see it. New York: Covici Friede, 1934.

Eisner, Elliot W. "Emerging models for educational evaluation," School Review (August 1972): 573-89.

Eisner, Elliot W. The arts, human development, and education. Berkeley, Calif.: McCutchan, 1976.

Eisner, Elliot W. Reading, the arts, and the creation of meaning. Reston, Va.: National Association for Education through Art, 1978.

Freud, Sigmund. The basic writings of Sigmund Freud, ed. A.A.Brill. New York: The Modern Library, 1938.

Gadamer, Hans-Georg. Truth and method. London: Sheed and Ward, 1975.

Galileo. Dialogues concerning the two new sciences, trans. H.Crew and A.de Salvio. New York: Dover, 1952.

Glaser, B.G., and A.L.Strauss. Discovery of grounded theory. Chicago: Aldine, 1967.

Glaser, B.G., and A.L.Strauss. "Discovery of substantive theory: A basic strategy underlying qualitative research," in: W.J. Filstead (ed.) Qualitative methodology: Firsthand involvement with the social world. Chicago: Markham Pub., 1970.

Goffman, Erving. The presentation of self in everyday life. New York: Doubleday, 1959.

Hegel, G.W.E. The phenomenology of mind, trans. J.B. Baillie. New York: Harper, repr. 1967.

Heidegger, Martin. Being and time, trans. J.Macquarrie and E.Robinson. New York: Harper, 1962.

Heisenberg, Werner. Philosophic problems of nuclear science. London: Faber and Faber, 1952.

Horning, T. The development of a model of the psychological processes which translate musical stimula-

118

tion into affective experience. Doctoral dissertation. Case Western Reserve University, 1982.

Hume, David. Of the standard of taste (1757). New York: Bobbs-Merrill, 1965.

Hume, David. Treatise on human nature (1739), 2 vols. London: Dent, 1911.

Huntsman, K.H. "Improvisational dramatic activities: Key to self-actualization?" Children's Theatre Review, 31, 2 (Spring 1982): 3-9.

Husserl, Edmund. Cartesian meditations, trans. D. Cairns. The Hague: Nijhoff, 1960.

Kant, Immanuel. On education, trans. A.Churston. London: K.Paul, Trench, Trubner, 1899.

Kant, Immanuel. Critique of judgement, trans. J.C.Meredith. Oxford: Oxford University Press, 1952.

Kant, Immanuel. Critique of practical reason, trans. L. W.Beck. Indianapolis: Bobbs-Merrill, 1956.

Kant, Immanuel. Critique of pure reason, trans. M.Muller. Garden City, New York: Doubleday, 1966.

Kase-Polisini, Judith (ed.) Creative drama in a developmental context. Lanham, MD.: University Press of America, 1985.

Kelly, Edward F. Curriculum evaluation and literary criticism: The explication of an analogy. Doctoral dissertation. University of Illinois at Urbana-Champaign, 1971.

Kerlinger, R. Behavioral research: A conceptual approach. New York: Holt, Rinehart and Winston, 1979.

Kierkegaard, Soren. Concluding unscientific postcript, trans. D.F.Swenson and W.Lowrie. Princeton: Princeton University Press, 1941.

Korzybski, Alfred. Science and sanity. Lakefield, Conn.: International Society for General Semantics, 4th ed., 1958.

119

Langer, Susanne K. Feeling and form. New York: Scribner's, 1953.

Langer, Susanne K. Mind: An essay on human feeling, 3 vols. Baltimore: Johns Hopkins Press, 1967-84.

Lazier, Gil, Brian Sutton-Smith and Douglas A.Zahn. "A systematic analysis of developmental differences in dramatic improvisational behaviour," Speech Monographs, 38, 3 (1971): 155-65.

Leibnitz, G.W. Philosophic writings, trans. M.Morris. New York: Dutton, 1934.

Locke, John. Philosophical works, trans. J.A.St.John, 2 vols. London: G.Bell, 1883.

Lyman, Stanford M., and Marvin B.Scott. The drama of social reality. New York: Oxford University Press, 1975.

Mann, John S. "Curriculum criticism," Curriculum Theory Network, 2 (Winter 1968-69): 2-14.

McCaslin, Nellie. Theatre for children in the United States: A history. Norman: University of Oklahoma Press, 1971.

McGregor, Lynn, M.Tate and K.Robinson. Learning through drama. London: Heinemann, 1977.

McLaren, Peter L. Education as ritual performance. Doctoral dissertation. University of Toronto, 1983.

McLaren, Peter L. Schooling as ritual performance. London: Routledge and Kegan Paul, 1986.

McLeod, John N. A survey of drama in post primary schools. Melbourne, Australia: Drama Resource Centre, 1978.

McLeod, John N. Assessment and evaluation in drama. Melbourne, Australia: Drama Resource Centre, 1981.

McLuhan, H.Marshall. Understanding media. London: Routledge, 1964.

McLuhan, H.Marshall, and Quentin Fiore. The medium is the massage. New York: Bantam, 1967.

McLuhan, H.Marshall, and Quentin Fiore. War and peace
    in the global village. New York: Bantam, 1968.

Madeja, Stanley S. All the arts for every child. St.
    Louis: CEMREL, 1973.

Madeja, Stanley S.(ed.) Yearbooks on research in arts
    and aesthetic education, 4 vols. St.Louis: CEMREL,
    1977-81.

Madeja, Stanley S. Aesthetic education research. Paper
    presented to the International Society for Educa-
    tion Through the Arts, Adelaide, 1978a.

Marcel, Gabriel. The philosophy of existence, trans. M.
    Harari. London: Harvill Press, 1948.

Marx, Karl. Das kapital (1867, 1885, 1895), trans. E.
    and C.Paul. London: Dent, 1930.

Mead, G.H. Mind, self and society. Chicago: University
    of Chicago Press, 1934.

Merrell, Floyd. Semiotic foundations. Bloomington: Ind-
    iana University Press, 1982.

Miller, David (ed.) Popper selections. Princeton: Prin-
    ceton University Press, 1985.

Muller, Herbert J. Science and criticism: The humanis-
    tic tradition in contemporary thought. New Haven:
    Yale University Press, 1943.

Nietzsche, Friedrich. Thus spake Zarathustra (1883-85),
    trans. R.J.Hollingdale. Harmondsworth: Penguin,
    1969.

Ontario, Government of. Dramatic arts: Intermediate and
    senior divisions. Toronto: Ministry of Education,
    1981.

Peavey, R.Vance (ed.) Natcon 9. Ottawa: Employment and
    Immigration Canada, 1985.

Pepper, Stephen C. World hypotheses. Berkeley: Univer-
    sity of California Press, 1942.

Piaget, Jean. Structuralism, trans. C.Maschler. New
    York: Harper, 1968.

Plato. Dialogues, trans. B.Jowett. Oxford: Oxford University Press, 1871.

Polanyi, Michael. Personal knowledge. New York: Harper and Row, 1964.

Popham, W.James. Objectives and instruction, AERA Monograph Series on Curriculum Evaluation, No.3. Chicago: Rand McNally, 1969: 32-52.

Ross, Malcolm (ed.) The arts: A way of knowing. Oxford: Pergamon, 1983.

Rousseau, Jean-Jacques. Emile, trans. B.Foxley. London: Dent (1911), 1943.

Rugg, Harold. Imagination. New York: Harper and Row, 1963.

Russell, Bertrand. Human knowledge. London: Allen and Unwin, 1948.

Sartre, Jean-Paul. The transcendance of the ego, trans. F.William and R.Kirkpatrick. New York: Farrar, Strauss and Cudahy, 1957.

Sartre, Jean-Paul. Sketch for a theory of emotions, trans. P.Mairet. London: Methuen, 1952.

Sartre, Jean-Paul. The psychology of imagination, trans. B.Frechtman. New York: Washington Square, repr. 1966a.

Sartre, Jean-Paul. Being and nothingness, trans. H.E. Barnes. New York: Washington Square, repr. 1966.

Scriven, Michael. The methodology of evaluation, AERA Monograph Series on Curriculum Evaluation, No.1. Chicago: Rand McNally, 1967: 39-83.

Shannon, Claude E. "A mathematical theory of information," Bell System Technical Journal, 27 (1948): 379-342, 623-56.

Shannon, Claude E. "The bandwagon," Institute of Electrical and Electronic Engineers, Transactions on Information Theory, 2, 3 (1956): 3.

Smith, Louis M., and Sally Schumacher. Extended pilot trials of the aesthetic education program: A qualitative description, analysis and evaluation. St. Louis: CEMREL, 1972.

Smith, Louis M., and Paul A.Pohland. Education, technology, and the rural highlands, AERA Monograph Series on Curriculum Evaluation, No.7. Chicago: Rand McNally, 1974.

Spariosu, Mihai. Literature, mimesis and play. Philadelphia: John Benjamin, 1982.

Spinoza, Benedict. The works of Spinoza, trans. R.H.M. Elwes, 2 vols. New York: Dover, 1951.

Spradley, J.P. Participant observation. New York: Holt, Rinehart and Winston, 1980.

Stake, Robert. Evaluating the arts in education. Columbus, Ohio: Charles E.Merrill, 1975.

Stake, Robert, and Craig Gjerde. An evaluation of TCITY, the Twin City Institute for Talented Youth, AERA Monograph Series on Curriculum Evaluation, No.7. Chicago: Rand McNally, 1974.

Turner, Victor W. The ritual process. Harmondsworth: Penguin, 1974.

Tyler, Ralph. Basic principles of curriculum and instruction. Chicago: University of Chicago, 1950.

Undank, Jack. Diderot: Inside, outside and in-between. Madison, WI: Coda Press, 1979.

Vaihinger, Hans. Philosophy of "as if," trans. C.K. Ogden. London: Kegan Paul, repr. 1966.

Valle, Robert S., and Mark King (eds.) Existential-phenomenological alternatives for psychology. New York: Oxford University Press, 1978.

Watson, John D. The double helix. New York: Atheneum, 1968.

Willis, George (ed.) Qualitative evaluation. Berkeley, Calif.: McCutchan, 1978.

Wilkinson, Joyce A. "On evaluation of involvement in developmental drama and its relationship to self-

monitoring and hemisphericity," Children's Theatre
Review, 2, 32 (April 1983): 15-19.

Witkin, Robert W. The intelligence of feeling. London:
Heinemann, 1974.

Wittgenstein, Ludwig.   Tractus-logico-philosophicus,
trans. D.F.Pears and B.F.McGuinness. London: Routledge and Kegan Paul, repr. 1969.

INDEX

126

Form(s), 35, 43,65, 101;
of feeling, 35; sym-
bolic, 35.
Foucault, Michel, 36.
Frame(s): of reference,
33, 49, 62; of
research, 52, 53-60,
66, 102.
Freud, Sigmund, 22, 36,
118.
Funding, 72, 73, 82, 83,
84, 86, 87, 90, 91,
98, 101, 102, 106.

Gadamer, Hans-Georg, 33,
118.
Galileo Galilei, 10, 15,
19, 118.
Gall, M.D., 56, 95, 100,
113.
General semantics/-ist(s),
28.
General Systems Theory,
28.
Glaser, B.G., 59, 118.
God, god(s), 11, 12, 18,
33, 39.
Goffman, Erving, 29, 118.
Goldoni, Carlo, 19.
Golsmith, Oliver, 19.
Greeks, 12; see also
Athens.
Greimas, A-J., 37.
Grounded theory, 59, 85,
87, 88, 90, 91, 94.
Guess/-ing, 26.
Gulbenkian Foundation,
72.

Halifax, 85.
Hamilton Philharmonic
Institute, 83-84.
Handicapped: learning,
89; mentally, 4, 108;
physically, 4, 108.
Harmonies, 36.
Hearing impaired, 111.
Hegel, G.W.E., 22, 35,
71, 118.
Heidegger, Martin, 20,

32-33, 76, 105, 118.
Heisenberg, Werner, 26,
118.
Heller, Jack, 19, 114.
Hemisphericity, 95-96.
Heraclitus, 13, 20, 21,
22, 28, 76, 105.
History, 13, 68.
Hoffa, Harlan, 73.
Holism/-ist(s), whole(s),
8, 12, 13, 19, 21, 22,
26, 30, 33, 42, 64,
82, 95, 103.
Homer, 13.
Horning, Thomas, 59, 118.
Hume, David, 18-19, 20,
71, 119.
Huntsmann, Karla H., 57.
Husserl, Edmund, 31, 34,
119.
Hypothesis/-theses/
-thetical, 30, 44,
58, 66, 75, 94, 97,
100, 102, 103; non-
hypothesized, 59; see
also Guess.

I and Thou, 34.
Idealism/-ist(s), 30, 35-
36.
Identities, 36.
Illusion(s), 10, 13, 18,
20.
Imagination/-ining,
images, 1, 34, 35, 39,
43, 49, 96.
Indeterminacy, see
Uncertainty.
Induction, see Logic.
Inference(s), 47, 49,
77.
Information, 29, 46, 96;
metaphor, 26-27.
Intention/-al/-ity, 31,
32.
Inter-action, 61, 75.
International history of
educational drama,
101.
Interpretation, 32.

Interview/-ing, 32, 57, 58, 59, 81, 85, 88, 96; unstructured, 32.
Intuition/-ive, 8, 18, 20, 35, 39, 41.
Inventive/-ness, invention, 3, 13, 89, 108.
Involvement, 95-96.

James, William, 30.
JDR IIIrd Fund, 73.
Jewish, 17, 33.
Joint Council on Education (Toronto), 90-92.
Judging/-ment(s), 3, 7, 20, 43, 47, 48, 49, 74, 76, 77, 80, 82, 103, 106; aims, 80; comparative, 80; content, 80; function, 80; non-comparative, 80; value, 96; worth, 80.

Kant, Immanuel, 9, 19-21, 31, 33, 34, 35, 76, 119.
Kase-Polisini, Judith, 77, 119.
Kelly, Edward, 76, 119.
Kennedy, John F., 72.
Keppel, Francis, 72.
Kettering Foundation, 73.
Kierkegaard, Soren, 32, 119.
King, Mark, 59, 123.
Knowing/-ledge, 1, 2, 7, 8, 9, 10, 11, 12, 13, 14, 17, 19, 20, 21, 23, 25, 26, 27, 28, 29, 32, 33, 34, 35, 37, 38, 39, 40-44, 45, 47, 48, 49, 50, 51, 53, 93, 96, 103; ABOUT, 40-41, 76, 107; abstract, 20; by acquaintance, 40; aesthetic, 20, 35, 37, 103; by description, 41; explicit, 41-44;

felt, 8; IN, 40-41, 107; intuitive, see Intuition; by kind, 40-41; know-how, 43; modern, 14-23; practical, 4, 41, 43-44, 49, 50, 52, 75, 82; religious, 11; scientific, 14-16; tacit, 41-44, 49; by type, 41-44.
Korzybski, A., 28, 55.
Kuzmich, Natalie, 90, 117.

Lacan, Jacques, 36.
Langer, Suzanne K., 35, 119.
Language(s), 8, 33, 36, 41, 42, 48; games, 33.
Lazier, Gil, 57, 120.
Learner(s), 2, 8, 15, 44, 76; see also Learning.
Learning(s), 7, 11, 19, 53, 76, 78, 79, 82, 87, 88, 89, 91, 94, 106; aesthetic, 3, 4, 37, 78, 102-03, 106; affective, 78, 103; cognitive, 78, 103; extrinsic, 3, 4; handicaps, 89; immediate, 78; intrinsic, 3, 4, 108; learning to learn, 3; long-term, multiple, 78; strategies, 72; transfer of, 3, 89; types of, 2-4; see also Learner.
"Learning Through the Arts" Project, 87-90, 94.
Leibnitz, G.W., 17-18, 20, 120.
Lévi-Strauss, Claude, 36.
Limitation(s), 38.
Locke, John, 16, 17-18, 19, 20, 120.
Logic/-al, 17, 18, 27, 32, 35, 37, 45-46, 48,

130

49, 67; classical,
46; contemporary, 46;
deductive, 13, 16,
44-45, 46, 57, 71;
inductive, 13, 15, 19,
23, 44-45, 46, 57, 71;
symbolic, 18.
Lowenfeld, Viktor, 72.
Luckman, Thomas, 26, 28,
113.
Lyman, Stanford M., 28,
120.

McCaslin, Nellie, 57,
120.
McGill University, 55.
McGregor, Lynn, 57, 120.
McLaren, Peter L., 99,
120.
McLeod, John N., 57, 120.
McLuhan, H.Marshall, 2,
8, 42, 105, 120.
Madeja, Stanley S., 31,
72, 73, 97, 120-21.
Manic-depressive, 111.
Mann, John, 76.
Map/territory, 28, 40,
42.
Marcel, Gabriel, 34, 121.
Marx, Karl, 22, 36, 121.
Mask, 32; see also Role.
Mass, The, 14.
Materials, 53.
Mead, G.H., 29, 30, 71,
121.
Meaning(s)/-ful, 1, 2, 8,
21, 29, 32, 33, 37,
43, 48, 49, 50, 105.
Measure(s)/-ment, 23, 37,
47, 74, 75, 93-95,
105; research, 93-95;
see also Statistics.
Mechanical/-ism/-ist(s),
2, 20, 21, 23, 25, 26,
32, 36, 37, 38, 46,
51, 62, 71, 82, 94,
109, 110; machine
metaphor, see Meta-
phor; mechanical
inquiry, 16-17.

Media/-tion/medium, 8,
28, 33, 48, 75; art,
1, 43, 92.
Medieval, 26; church, 9,
10; research, 14;
world view, 14.
Melbourne, 73; State Col-
lege, 86-87.
Merrell, Floyd, 37, 121.
Mesopotamia(n), 11.
Message, 27, 28.
Metaphor(s)/-ical(ly),
14, 29, 37, 42, 43,
75, 77, 103; bodily,
42; dramatic, 27-29;
information, 26-27;
machine, 16-17, 18,
22, 25, 26; of mind,
23; structure, 42.
Method(s)/-ology/
-ological, 37, 38, 39,
43, 45, 52, 53, 61,
64, 77, 80, 81, 82,
85, 88, 91, 93, 94,
105, 109, 111; desc-
riptive, 56-57; his-
torical, 55, 56-58,
59; philosophical, 56,
58, 59; research, 56-
60; thesis, 55-56, 61,
64, 66, 68; see Expe-
rimental; Grounded
Theory.
Mill, John Stuart, 15,
23, 71, 76.
Miller, David, 50, 121.
Model(s), 13, 14, 28, 29,
38, 59, 76, 81.
Modern: inquiry, 23;
knowing, 14-23.
Montreal, 55.
Moore, G.E., 37.
Moral(s)/-ity, 19, 21,
45; reasons, 45.
Morrison, Jack, 86.
Motivation, 3, 36, 89,
108.
Movement, 96.
Muller, Herbert J., 27,
121.

Multivariate research, 60.
Music/-ian(s), 2, 5, 12, 47, 48, 54, 60, 64, 72, 73, 83-84, 88, 89, 91, 94, 97; therapy, 107, 110, 111; see also Singing.
Mystery, 13; cycles, 14; religion, 12.
Myth, 11, 13, 14, 26, 36; see also Ritual.

Narrative, 57.
Naturalism/-tic, 7, 21, 22, 57, 58.
Nature, la belle, 20.
Near East, ancient, 101.
Neill, A.S., 7.
New Zealand, 4.
Newton, Sir Isaac, 9, 16, 17, 18, 19, 38.
19th century inquiry, 21-23.
Nothingness, 32, 35.

Objective(s)/-ly/-ity, 1, 2, 7, 13, 14, 15, 17, 18, 19, 26, 32, 44, 46, 49, 65, 72, 74, 75, 77, 80, 83, 94, 100, 101; expressive objectives, 76; see also Subjective.
Observer/-ation(al), 15, 17, 19, 26, 31, 34, 39, 46, 57, 61, 75, 81, 82, 88, 99, 100, 101; direct, 32; participant, 59; unobserved observer, 32.
Ontario, 64, 73, 79, 81, 87-90, 91.
Ontario Arts Council, 83.
Ontario Institute for Studies in Education, 55, 90-92.
Ontological/-ogy, 20.
Opposition(s), 37.
Oscillate/-tion, 42.

Park, Paul, 87, 108, 117.
Participant observation, 59, 87.
Pavlov, Ivan, 15.
Peavey, R.Vance, 59, 121.
Peirce, C.S., 30.
Pennsylvania State University, 72.
Pepper, Stephen C., 9, 121.
Percept/-ion/-ual, 3, 89, 92, 108.
Performance, 33, 83, 99.
Personal record/diary, 59.
Perspective(s), 7, 28, 29, 34, 39, 45, 51, 58, 65, 75, 84, 94; dramaturgical, 28; individual, 34; new, 58; philosophic, 30-37; relative, 25-29.
Phenomena/-on/-ology/ -ologist(s), 20, 30, 31-32, 51, 57, 58, 59, 68, 83; phenomenological reduction, 31.
Philosophic inquiry, 17-19, 56, 58, 59, 68, 82, 101-02.
Piaget, Jean/Piagetian, 8, 35, 36, 64, 121.
Picasso, Pablo, 106.
Pirandello, Luigi, 21.
Plato, 13, 20, 21, 35, 121.
Play, 22, 28, 33, 34, 36, 105; aesthetic, 35; of appearances, 21; fictions, 21, 33; player, 25, 32, 33; world, 28, 33, 42-43, 76, 105.
Plays, 19; see also Drama.
Poetry, 5, 16.
Polanyi, Michael, 41, 121.
Polarities, 36; see also Binary; Duality.
Policy, 81, 87.

Pope, Alexander, 19.
Popham, James, 74, 122.
Popper, Sir Karl, 39, 47,
    48, 50.
Possession/-essed, 12, 13.
Post-structuralism/
    -ist(s), 37; see also
    Structuralism.
Power, 10, 11.
Practical/-ity, 16, 19,
    20, 21, 23, 47; prac-
    tical knowledge, see
    Knowledge.
Pragmatism/-ist(s), 30-31,
    35, 51.
Praxis, 51.
Pre-Socratic(s), 13, 21.
Priest(s), 11, 12, 13, 14.
Probability/-ies, 16, 26,
    27.
Problem/-atic, ix, 52, 62,
    64, 66, 68.
Problem identification,
    63, 64, 100.
Problem-solving, 3, 7, 30,
    47, 63, 64, 89, 108.
Process(es), 28, 30, 42,
    43, 78, 79, 86, 96,
    101.
Progressivism/-ist(s),
    7-8.
Program(s): arts, 34, 48,
    77 (special, 89); de-
    sign, 89; general, 2-4,
    87-90; implementation,
    59, 89, 92, 108; integ-
    rated arts, 90; music,
    47; P/J, 87-90; plan-
    ning 59; pre-professio-
    nal 4; special, 108;
    specialized, 4; speci-
    fic, 92, types of, 4-5;
    see Evaluation.
Protestant/-ism, 16.
Proust, Marcel, 61.
Psychology, 35, 36, 51,
    55, 94, 109, 110;
    developmental, 8;
    experimental, 74.
Puritan(s), 16.

Pythagoras, 9, 12.

Qualitative/quality, 23,
    35, 47, 58, 60, 77,
    78, 82, 83, 99, 102,
    109; see also Evalua-
    tion.
Quantify/quantification,
    15, 93, 96.
Quantitative/quantity,
    23, 35, 37, 46, 47,
    58, 60, 76, 77, 78,
    82, 90, 95, 102, 109;
    see also Evaluation.
Questionnare(s), 57, 58,
    64, 96.

Rational, see Reason.
Ratke, Wolfgang, 19.
Read, Herbert, 7.
Reading, 3, 94, 110.
Reagan, Ronald, 73.
Realism/-ist(s), 30, 37.
Reason(s)/-ing/rational,
    8, 14, 18, 20, 21, 39,
    43, 44-48, 50, 51, 93,
    94, 100, 103, 105; de-
    ductive, inductive,
    see Logic; interpreta-
    tive, moral, 45, 49;
    objective, see Objec-
    tive; styles of, 44-
    45.
Reber, Arthur S., 42,
    113.
Red Deer, Alberta, 98.
Redundancy, 27.
Reflection/reflexivity,
    19, 29, 35, 36, 76.
Relative/-ity, 30, 47,
    49, 78; effect of, 25-
    29.
Religion/-ious, 10, 11,
    12, 17.
Renaissance, 14.
Research (projects), 93-
    103; developmental
    drama scale, 95-96;
    field, 98-100; histo-
    rical, 100-101;

135

Tyler, Ralph, 72, 74, 123.
Uncertainty, 26, 27; see
   also Certainty.
Uniqueness, 3.
United States, 4, 5, 7,
   54, 71, 72-73, 74, 82,
   97, 99.
University of New Mexico,
   86.
University of Toronto,
   90-92.
Use, Utilitarianism, 19,
   23, 82.

Vaihinger, Hans, 27, 123.
Valle, Robert S., 59, 123.
Value(s), 7-8, 14, 15,
   26, 34, 38, 62, 75,
   78, 80, 88, 96; aesthetic, 47; knowledge-
   value, 35; see also
   Assumptions; Beliefs.
Vancouver, 85.
Vancouver Island, 11.
Victoria, B.C., 55.
Vienna, 33.
Visual art(s), 5, 7, 8,
   48, 54, 59, 60, 72,
   73, 88, 89, 91, 94,
   97; teacher associa-
   tion, 89; therapy,
   107, 110.
Voltaire, Francois, 19.

Watson, J.B., 15, 71.
Watson, John D., 27, 123.
Way, Brian, 65.
Whitehead, A.N., 22.
Whole, see Holism.
Wilkinson, Joyce A., 95-
   96, 123.
Will, George F., 53.
Willis, George, 77, 123.
Winnipeg, 85.
Witkin, Robert W., 35-36,
   123.
Wittgenstein, Ludwig, 33,
   37, 45, 47, 124.
Work, 16.
World: actual, 42-43;
   aesthetic, 42-43, 76;
   classical, 12-14; fic-
   tional, see Fiction;
   play, 42-43, 76, 105.
World view, 9, 14.
Writing, 13.
Wrong, Being, 47-48.

Xenophanes, 20.

136

THE AUTHOR

Professor Richard Courtney supervises graduate work, research and development in arts education at the Ontario Institute for Studies in Education. He is cross-appointed to the Graduate Centre for Study of Drama, University of Toronto.

A leading authority in drama and arts education, he is also well-known for works on ritual drama and aesthetic theory. He has over 150 publications of which 8 books are currently in print:

Play, Drama & Thought
The Rarest Dream: 'Play, Drama & Thought' Re-Visited
Re-Play
The Dramatic Curriculum
Drama In Therapy (with Gertrud Schattner) 2 vols
Outline History of British Drama
&
Teacher Education in the Arts
Basic Books in Arts Education
(both with David Booth, John Emerson & Natalie Kuzmich)